EVIDENCE SIMULATIONS

Second Edition

Fred Galves
Professor of Law

Edward J. Imwinkelried
Professor of Law Emeritus
University of California, Davis School of Law

Thomas J. Leach
Professor of Law
University of the Pacific—McGeorge School of Law

BRIDGE TO PRACTICE®

WEST ACADEMIC PUBLISHING

444 Cedar Street, Suite 700
St. Paul, MN 55101
1-877-888-1330

Printed in the United States of America

ISBN: 978-1-64020-099-9

TABLE OF CONTENTS

Evidence Simulations

Second Edition

INTRODUCTION

I. BACKGROUND

This *Bridge to Practice* Series is premised on the idea that in-class simulations are of value to students, professors, and employers in three important ways: (1) simulations will deepen students' grasp of the underlying principles and rules in a given doctrinal area; (2) internalizing the subject matter will enable the class to accelerate study of a particular topic; and (3) notably for the "bridge" aspect of this series, students will enter the practice of law with more experience in performing the professional tasks and activities that lawyers actually execute—they will be more "practice-ready," just as doctors are more "practice ready" if while in medical school they actually treat patients, in addition to reading textbooks and attending class lectures.[1] Perhaps more than in any other subject regularly covered in law-school study and on bar exams, use of frequent simulations in the study of Evidence law can yield these benefits.

First, the study of Evidence requires close analysis of specific rules, and this often leads to a myopic, "micro" view of the issue in question: Can the judge be persuaded the evidence is "needlessly cumulative" to qualify for exclusion under FRE 403? Does the proffered testimony constitute inadmissible "character" evidence under FRE 404? In the real-life way that evidence questions arise in courtrooms, the questions do not exist in a vacuum. Whether evidence is "cumulative" depends on how much other similar evidence there is; whether it is "needless" requires not only a consideration of the effect of all the other similar evidence but also an assessment of the challenged item of evidence's importance relative to the other evidence. What seems at first to be propensity evidence may alternatively be admissible as non-character evidence of a "plan" or "modus operandi" under FRE 404(b), when viewed in conjunction with other evidence. The student who views a 403 or 404 issue using the tunnel vision of simple mechanical rule application, without regard to the overall trial context, will miss these subtleties. Simply stated, she will end up with an incomplete grasp of how the rules work in actual practice.

But—and here is the first connection to simulations—it is hard to see the context of a particular piece of evidence, that is, the operation of that item of evidence in the sweep of the trial, *when there is no trial*. That is why many law schools[2] have instituted "integrated" courses that combine teaching the substantive law of evidence and trial advocacy skills: the latter provides the context for the former. However, such courses are

[1] This third value is a reflection of the importance placed by the Carnegie Foundation's study, *Educating Lawyers: Preparation for the Profession of Law* (2007), on altering law-school curricula to provide training in practical skills, to replace the disappearing mentoring system.

[2] Pacific McGeorge and Temple University, for example, are among the law schools that have integrated Trial Advocacy and Evidence in this way to promote learning and reinforcement in both disciplines.

faculty-intensive and expensive. For schools that rely on the standard "podium"-style course to teach evidence, the simulations in this book offer a substitute for a full trial-advocacy component. Similarly, the practice pointers on Evidence in this book provide a refresher for students in Trial Advocacy who must recall Evidence concepts from either a past class or who are enrolled in an Evidence course simultaneously.

Second, it is often difficult to recognize an evidentiary issue when it comes along in "real life" until one has seen it, heard it, and felt its effects in actual operation. The ability to recognize objections on the fly is an experiential skill that can be acquired only by practice and repetition. Every beginning trial lawyer we know has had this experience: she comes home from her first full day of trial, reviews the daily transcript she spent a fortune to get that night, and cringes when she sees in cold print 15 items of damaging hearsay evidence that came in without a peep of objection from her. Why? Was it because she did not learn what hearsay was in law school or she failed the evidence segment of the bar exam? No—in her sleep she can recite (and tonight, tossing and turning before Trial Day 2, she surely will rehearse), "Hearsay is an out-of-court statement offered to prove the truth of the matter asserted." She might even know a plainer-English formulation like: "To determine if the out-of-court statement violates the hearsay ban, ask yourself: Do we have to assess the credibility of the declarant in order to use it for the purpose it is offered?" But neither of these incantations helped her during Day 1, and they are unlikely to aid her much on Day 2, *because she has never encountered hearsay in the flesh.* She may know the formal definition of hearsay, but she will likely fail to recognize it in the applied setting of a trial if she has not learned it "experientially."

An in-class simulation provides the beginnings of the experience necessary to be alert to object to hearsay when it rears its ugly head. A student who has acted the part of opposing counsel in a dramatization in which the questioning lawyer asks, "What did the bystander tell you about which car had the red light?" is better prepared than the student who has seen this issue only in a multiple-choice[3] or essay question. That is never how evidentiary issues arise in practice.

II. CASE FILES AND EXERCISES IN THIS BOOK

In the Appendix, you will find the outline and components of two short case files that provide the material for all the exercises for each topic of Evidence. Read these case files and thumbnail summaries several times

[3] Many multiple-choice questions suffer from a defect beyond the fact that they are not "live": they use indirect rather than direct quotes. For example, the question might be "If the questioning lawyer asks the witness to recite what a bystander told her about which car had the red light, the court should rule. . . ." It would be closer to "live" to write: "If the questioning lawyer asks, 'Mr. Witness, what did the bystander tell you about which car had the red light?' the court should rule. . . ." However, while such written formulations can be helpful in exploring hearsay in the abstract, a truly "live" enactment of the courtroom scene will be better than either, as it requires an immediate, extemporaneous response using verbal analysis and argument expressed in an articulate and persuasive manner.

over so that you are fully familiar with the facts, the parties' claims and defenses, and the applicable law set out in the Jury Instructions.[4]

The volume is divided into ten chapters, each covering a major topic of Evidence law. Each chapter contains one or more exercises that your professor may assign you for preparation and presentation in class. Each exercise is prefaced by a short introduction ("Tips and Pointers") discussing practical aspects of the topic of evidence covered. These introductions are *not* intended to teach you the law of the topic; that task falls to your other assigned readings and in-class work with your professor and classmates.[5] Instead, the introduction is designed to give you working "tips" on how to handle the issue presented—for example, the standard "lingo" the judge may expect, methods of making supporting and opposing arguments more persuasive, and pitfalls to avoid. Your professor may provide supplementary or different instructions; in that case, give the professor what he or she wants, just as you must give your judge what he or she wants!

Here are some general observations about how to make the exercises more realistic.

- Enter into the role-playing aspect of the exercise. Imagine that you are arguing a pretrial in limine motion to a judge or are actually in the moment at trial. The person on the stand is your witness or an opposing witness to whose testimony you are assigned to object; or that you are arguing to the appellate court reviewing a trial-court evidentiary ruling. Your professor may arrange the classroom to simulate a courtroom layout and might even request courtroom attire in order to make it feel more like a trial.

- Perform the exercise in present-tense, real-time role play. For example, when arguing your support for or opposition to an item of evidence, do not say: "Your Honor, *we would argue that* this testimony qualifies as a present sense impression under 803(1). . . ." You ARE arguing, so say: "Your Honor, the witness is testifying to his present sense impression under 803(1)—his out-of-court statement was made while observing the event that he was describing at the time." It is important to remain in role. Try not to break role, even if you make a mistake and want to discuss it immediately. *Be bold and definitive.* Do not say: "Objection—isn't this hearsay?" Say forcefully: "Objection, hearsay!" (The exclamation point is intended to convey the resolute sound of your voice.) Be confident in your position and sound as if you believe your own argument. (There is an alternative you may hear in

[4] In courses in which the professor has decided to teach Evidence integrated with Trial Advocacy, the students may also be assigned the longer, full-text versions of either or both case files, which should then be used in addition to the summaries included in this volume.

[5] *See, e.g.*, Beckman, Crump & Galves, *Evidence: A Contemporary Approach*, 3d Ed. (West 2016) (providing checklists, sample transcripts, chapter summaries, call-out box commentary on cases, and online resources).

court, as if it added something: "Rank [or classic] hearsay!" We do not recommend this; see the ensuing discussion of "empty rhetoric.")

- Try to anticipate what your opponent is likely to argue. Have in mind—preferably in your trial notes—a decision tree: "If opponent argues the time lapse was too long for a present sense impression under 803(1), respond with (a) a few minutes is not too long, as it is unlikely that the quality of the declarant's memory deteriorated or the declarant had enough time to formulate a lie, so the hearsay rule's concern with trustworthiness is satisfied. (b) Alternatively, this is an excited utterance under 803(2). Be prepared to lay the foundation to show that declarant was still stressed and excited from the startling event. . . ." In short, you should have a "Plan B" or another line of defense. As they say in the military, have contingency plans.
- Avoid empty rhetoric—*i.e.*, words that add nothing substantive to the persuasive power of your argument beyond making it longer. The typical trial judge is impatient; her time is a precious commodity, and she wants you to get right to the point. If you offer evidence to which your opponent objects, "Irrelevant," you lose points with the judge if your retort starts, "You Honor, we *feel* this evidence is highly relevant." First, your feelings are unimportant—a trial is not a therapy session. Is the evidence relevant or not? Second, the judge already knows you consider it relevant: that is why you are offering it.[6] Third, your task is to explain to the judge *how* and *why* the evidence is relevant, which entails tying your argument directly to the facts and the language of Rule 401: "This testimony about purchases of lighter fluid makes it more likely that the defendant was planning the acts of arson with which he is charged." Whenever possible, quote the controlling language of the rule. Policy is soft. In contrast, statutory language is much harder. Take the high ground of the statutory text.
- Finally—but perhaps most importantly for those students who have not seen a real trial or taken a trial-skills course—here are three fundamentals of trials:
  - The overall order of events:
    1. Preliminary matters/motions
    2. Jury selection
    3. Plaintiff's/prosecution's opening statement
    4. Defendant's opening statement (it may be reserved until beginning of defense case)

[6] This presumes, of course, that the judge has not formed a jaundiced view of your *bona fides* and/or your grasp of Evidence law. We trust that presumption will result from your faithful practice of the exercises in this book.

5. P's case-in-chief: witnesses (direct exam/cross exam), exhibits
6. D's case-in-chief (if a counterclaim) or defense-in chief: witnesses (direct exam/cross exam), exhibits
7. P's rebuttal case
8. D's surrebuttal or rejoinder case
9. P's closing argument or summation (opening)[7]
10. D's closing argument or summation
11. P's rebuttal argument or summation
12. Judge's instructions giving jury the law to apply and instructions for deliberations

- The order of examination of each witness:
  1. Direct examination of the witness
  2. Cross-examination of the witness
  3. Redirect examination
  4. Re-cross examination
- The form of questions:

  The vast majority of the objections that arise at trial relate to the form of the question rather than substantive evidentiary doctrines such as hearsay. In this short text, we cannot go into as much detail as Capra & Greenberg, *The Form of the Question: Texts, Material and Exercises on the Evidentiary Rules of Form* (2014), but we hope to give you some exposure to the major form problems. Under FRE 611(c) and state-law equivalents, leading questions are generally forbidden on direct and redirect. However, they are allowed on cross and re-cross of the opponent's witnesses and on direct when the direct examiner calls "a hostile witness, an adverse party, or a witness identified with an adverse party." The more difficult task for beginning trial lawyers is recognizing the difference between a non-leading and a leading question on the fly at trial. This will be important for you to understand for the simulation exercises, as you will be conducting many directs and crosses. Here is a start, which your professor will undoubtedly expand on during the course.

  1. The best form of non-leading question on direct is "open-ended," allowing the witness relatively free rein in answering and NOT suggesting the answer. These questions typically start with: WHO – WHAT – WHERE – WHEN – HOW – WHY – WHICH – DESCRIBE – TELL

[7] In some jurisdictions, summations are done in only two stages: D closes first, followed by P. There is no "rebuttal" argument.

US. Be conscious of the *first word out of your mouth* at the beginning of the question. When you have a good witness, you want to put the witness's honesty and intelligence on optimal display for the jury. The best way to do that is to use non-leading questions to encourage the witness to open up and talk to the jury.

2. Closed-ended questions, which usually begin with "Did you . . .?" or "Was there . . .?" point more toward the answer, or at least the subject matter, aimed at by the questioner. Such questions may or may not be impermissibly leading on direct, depending on how clearly they signal the answer. "Did you do anything else to check on the defendant's state of sobriety?" is likely not objectionably leading. But "Did you give the defendant three field sobriety tests, all of which he failed, to determine that he was legally intoxicated?" will surely be ruled objectionably leading.

3. The best form of leading question on cross, however, is not simply closed-ended. Instead, it is a non-argumentative statement of the fact the cross-examiner intends to elicit, converted into a question by means of a "tag" such as "correct?" or "that is right?" or even a simple "yes?" It clearly suggests the answer. "Before you arrested the defendant for DUI, you did more, didn't you?" "You administered field sobriety tests, isn't that right?" "In fact, you did three such tests, yes?" These questions demand the desired answer from the adverse witness, not simply point towards it. For that reason, most trial-skills teachers will not be satisfied if you ask on cross, "Didn't you administer three FSTs to the defendant." In the words of one renowned such teacher, "Counsel, on cross, don't ask—tell." As Albert Krieger, the former president of the National Association of Criminal Defense Lawyers, famously remarked: "In good cross, you really do not ask questions. Under the guise of asking questions, you make factual statements on the record and force the witness to assent."

4. Finally, think of the cross-examination of a hostile witness as a type of closing argument in which you "footnote" each point/sentence that you make in argument with authoritative references. Those authoritative references are the witness's answers to your leading questions.

Please keep these general points in mind when addressing the problems in this book. To that end, in Chapter 1, we provide various transcript examples of lawyers questioning witnesses that can serve as helpful guides when formulating questions for witnesses. We hope you enjoy these exercises. Simulated trial work is fun and satisfying—you begin assuming your professional role as an attorney. It is the only way you can develop the expertise and skill required to become a competent trial attorney. Moreover, you will understand Evidence law all the better when you have actively "done it" and "lived it."

CHAPTER 1

QUESTIONING WITNESSES

I. TIPS & POINTERS: BASIC WITNESS EXAMINATIONS

Rule 601. Competency to Testify in General

Every person is competent to be a witness unless these rules provide otherwise. But in a civil case, state law governs the witness's competency regarding a claim or defense for which state law supplies the rule of decision.

Rule 602. Need for Personal Knowledge

A witness may testify to a matter only if evidence is introduced sufficient to support a finding that the witness has personal knowledge of the matter. Evidence to prove personal knowledge may consist of the witness's own testimony. This rule does not apply to a witness's expert testimony under Rule 703.

Rule 603. Oath or Affirmation to Testify Truthfully

Before testifying, a witness must give an oath or affirmation to testify truthfully. It must be in a form designed to impress that duty on the witness's conscience.

. . .

Rule 607. Who May Impeach a Witness

Any party, including the party that called the witness, may attack the witness's credibility.

Rule 610. Religious Beliefs or Opinions

Evidence of a witness's religious beliefs or opinions is not admissible to attack or support the witness's credibility.

Rule 611. Mode and Order of Examining Witnesses and Presenting Evidence

(a) **Control by the Court; Purposes.** The court should exercise reasonable control over the mode and order of examining witnesses and presenting evidence so as to:

(1) make those procedures effective for determining the truth;

(2) avoid wasting time; and

(3) protect witnesses from harassment or undue embarrassment.

(b) Scope of Cross-Examination. Cross-examination should not go beyond the subject matter of the direct examination and matters affecting the witness's credibility. The court may allow inquiry into additional matters as if on direct examination.

(c) Leading Questions. Leading questions should not be used on direct examination except as necessary to develop the witness's testimony. Ordinarily, the court should allow leading questions:

(1) on cross-examination; and

(2) when a party calls a hostile witness, an adverse party, or a witness identified with an adverse party.

Rule 612. Writing Used to Refresh a Witness

(a) Scope. This rule gives an adverse party certain options when a witness uses a writing to refresh memory:

(1) while testifying; or

(2) before testifying, if the court decides that justice requires the party to have those options.

(b) Adverse Party's Options; Deleting Unrelated Matter. Unless 18 U.S.C. § 3500 provides otherwise in a criminal case, an adverse party is entitled to have the writing produced at the hearing, to inspect it, to cross-examine the witness about it, and to introduce in evidence any portion that relates to the witness's testimony. If the producing party claims that the writing includes unrelated matter, the court must examine the writing in camera, delete any unrelated portion, and order that the rest be delivered to the adverse party. Any portion deleted over objection must be preserved for the record.

(c) Failure to Produce or Deliver the Writing. If a writing is not produced or is not delivered as ordered, the court may issue any appropriate order. But if the prosecution does not comply in a criminal case, the court must strike the witness's testimony or—if justice so requires—declare a mistrial.

Rule 613. Witness's Prior Statement

(a) Showing or Disclosing the Statement During Examination. When examining a witness about the witness's prior statement, a party need not show it or disclose its contents to the witness. But the party must, on request, show it or disclose its contents to an adverse party's attorney.

(b) Extrinsic Evidence of a Prior Inconsistent Statement. Extrinsic evidence of a witness's prior inconsistent statement is admissible only if the witness is given an opportunity to explain or deny the statement and an adverse party is given an opportunity to examine the witness about it, or if justice so requires. This subdivision (b) does not apply to an opposing party's statement under Rule 801(d)(2).

Rule 614. Court's Calling or Examining a Witness

(a) Calling. The court may call a witness on its own or at a party's request. Each party is entitled to cross-examine the witness.

(b) Examining. The court may examine a witness regardless of who calls the witness.

(c) Objections. A party may object to the court's calling or examining a witness either at that time or at the next opportunity when the jury is not present.

Rule 615. Excluding Witnesses

At a party's request, the court must order witnesses excluded so that they cannot hear other witnesses' testimony. Or the court may do so on its own. But this rule does not authorize excluding:

(a) a party who is a natural person;

(b) an officer or employee of a party that is not a natural person, after being designated as the party's representative by its attorney;

(c) a person whose presence a party shows to be essential to presenting the party's claim or defense; or

(d) a person authorized by statute to be present.

Before beginning the experiential learning, or "learn-by-doing," exercises in this evidence simulations book, students first should practice the questioning of witnesses. Thus, the purpose of this foundational chapter is to familiarize the student with some rudimentary, yet critical, witness examination techniques used by competent trial attorneys. To accomplish this objective, various transcript samples of witness examinations are set forth below. These samples can serve as basic models for the student when questioning witnesses.

Article VI of the Federal Rules sets out many of the basic restrictions on the examination of witnesses. With Rules 601–615 in mind, consider the following samples as you begin to draft your own lines of questioning. After reviewing these samples, you will be asked to question witnesses by using these samples as template guides for your examinations.

The following discussion and question-answer samples are taken from: Syd Beckman, Susan Crump & Fred Galves, *Evidence: A Contemporary Approach*, (West Academic Publishers 3d ed. 2016). More specifically, the samples are drawn from Chapter 2 of that course book, "Sources of Evidence: Witnesses," ("Evidence Casebook"). The page numbers from that casebook chapter are referenced at the beginning of each sample examination:

➢ WITNESS COMPETENCY—R. 601

At trial, the threshold question is competency—that is, whether the person is qualified to give any testimony at all in the case. At common law, to be a competent witness, a person had to possess four testimonial capacities: perception, memory, narration, and sincerity.

Evidence Casebook, pp. 50–51

A Sample Foundation for Establishing a Child's Competency to Testify

If an opponent were to object to a child's competency, the proponent must show that the child recognizes a duty to tell the truth and can observe and coherently narrate events. In a case where a child has observed the plaintiff slip and fall at a grocery store, the questioning might be as follows:

Plaintiff's Attorney:	I call to the stand Matthew Olsen.
Defense Attorney:	I object, Your Honor. Matthew Olsen is a five-year-old child and incompetent to testify.
Plaintiff's Attorney:	Your Honor, I would like to lay a foundation for his testimony, if the court will permit me to.
Judge:	Request granted.
Plaintiff's Attorney:	What is your name?
Child Witness:	Matthew.
Plaintiff's Attorney:	Do you have a last name?
Child Witness:	Yes. Olsen.
Plaintiff's Attorney:	How old are you?
Child Witness:	Five.
Plaintiff's Attorney:	Do you know what it means to tell the truth?
Child Witness:	Yep. The truth is what really happens.
Plaintiff's Attorney:	Do you know what will happen to you if you do not tell the truth here today?
Child Witness:	Mommy and daddy will get real mad, and the devil will get me.
Plaintiff's Attorney:	You swore to tell the truth here today. Do you know what will happen if you don't?
Child Witness:	Yep. The judge will punish me.
Plaintiff's Attorney:	Do you remember what you did when you got up this morning?

Child Witness:	I went to the kitchen, and mommy fixed me cereal to eat.
Plaintiff's Attorney:	What happened next?
Child Witness:	I watched cartoons on the television.
Plaintiff's Attorney:	Do you remember what cartoons you watched?
Child Witness:	Marvel Avengers. I like Spiderman.
Plaintiff's Attorney:	And then what happened after you watched cartoons?
Child Witness:	I went into my bedroom and got dressed. And then I came here.
Plaintiff's Attorney:	Your Honor, I believe I have established that Matthew knows he has a duty to tell the truth, knows what the truth is, and can coherently observe and narrate events.
Judge:	I agree. The objection is overruled.

[There is a split of authority over the proper interpretation of Rule 601. If read literally, Rule 601 abolishes all competency requirements. The Advisory Committee Note to Rule 601 appears to confirm that the drafters meant precisely that. However, many courts have balked at adopting that radical reading of Rule 601. These latter courts treat Rule 601 as merely creating a rebuttable presumption of competency. However, even in the latter type of jurisdiction, the court might require that the opponent interpose any competency objection before the witness takes the oath; if the court imposed that procedural requirement, in the above example the competency objection would have been waived because Matthew has already been sworn. Assuming that there has been no waiver, the witness's proponent might then conduct the above sample examination. If the court subscribed to the latter interpretation of Rule 601, the court might permit the opposing attorney to conduct a voir dire—a mini-cross-examination of the prospective witness—in support of the objection. The voir dire would be strictly limited to the elements of the person's competency as a witness, e.g., perception, memory, narration, and sincerity.]

➢ PERSONAL KNOWLEDGE—R. 602

Evidence Casebook, pp. 65–66

A Sample Foundation for Establishing the Personal Knowledge of a Witness

Plaintiff's Attorney:	What is your name, please?
Witness:	My name is Claire Johnson.

Plaintiff's Attorney:	And what is your occupation?
Witness:	I am a high school algebra teacher.
Plaintiff's Attorney:	I want to take you back to an event that happened on Monday, January 21, 2014, at Campbell's grocery store at about 4:30 p.m., and ask if anything unusual happened at that time which you observed?
Witness:	Yes, I saw an older woman slip and fall because she pulled hard on some grocery carts.
Plaintiff's Attorney:	Where were you standing at the time you observed the slip and fall?
Witness:	I was about five feet away, waiting to get a cart.
Plaintiff's Attorney:	How well could you see the slip and fall from where you were standing?
Witness:	I was looking right at the woman.
Plaintiff's Attorney:	How well do you remember the slip and fall?
Witness:	Really well.
Plaintiff's Attorney:	Why?
Witness:	Because it happened right in front of me, and it was the only time I ever saw someone fall like that in the grocery store.
Plaintiff's Attorney:	Do you recognize anyone in the courtroom here today as the person whom you saw slip and fall on that occasion?
Witness:	Yes, the woman who sat next to you dressed in a yellow blouse.
Plaintiff's Attorney:	Your Honor, may the record reflect the witness has identified the plaintiff in this case, Gloria Miller.
Judge:	The record will so reflect.

[Rule 601 addresses the threshold question of whether the person is competent give any testimony at all in the case. Even if the person is competent, there are additional restrictions on the witness's testimony. Rule 602 imposes one of the most fundamental requirements, namely, that lay witnesses have firsthand knowledge of the facts and events that they testify to. Under Rule 602, the witness's own testimony can satisfy the foundational requirement. Rule 602 applies the lax, Rule 104(b) conditional relevance standard: The judge makes a limited inquiry; the judge asks only whether if the jury decides to believe the witness's testimony, the jury could rationally infer that the witness has personal, firsthand knowledge. However, it is often a mistake to lay a minimal, Rule 104(b) foundation. Especially if the witness is testifying to a central event on the historical merits of the case, the proponent should lay an extensive foundation showing that: The witness had an excellent opportunity to observe, the witness in fact observed, and at trial the witness presently recalls what he or she observed. Whenever possible, the proponent should elicit the witness's testimony that there was a special reason why the event imprinted so well in the witness's long-term memory. Note that in the above example, the witness testified that this was "the only time" the witness had observed such an event.]

➢ DIRECT EXAMINATION

Evidence Casebook, pp. 71–72

The following example illustrates the direct examination of a witness to an automobile accident. Notice several things about this line of questioning. (1) How the lawyer sets up and directs the witness and then slowly draws out the story piece by piece without having the witness tell his story all at once; (2) How the lawyer presents the witness's testimony in a logical, understandable and organized manner, occasionally summarizing important testimony in order to emphasize it; and (3) How questions are short, open-ended and often preceded by the words "**who**," "**what**," **"which,"** "**where**," "**when**," "**why**," and "**how**." These are natural interrogatory words—the words we resort to in a conversation when we are seeking information from the person we are talking to. When a direct examination question begins with one of these words, it is typically a proper, non-leading question under Rule 611(c). At various judicial education programs throughout the country, newly appointed judges are trained to listen to the first word of questions on direct examination. If the question does not begin in that fashion, the judge will be on alert for leading objections. Perhaps even more importantly, when you have a good witness, using non-leading phrases invites the witness to open up to the jury and put her honesty and intelligence on optimal display. The jury wants to hear the witness's version of the facts, not the attorney's.

Plaintiff's Attorney: Mr. Witness, **where** were you standing when the collision occurred?

Witness: I was standing on Main and Fifth Streets.

Plaintiff's Attorney: **Why** were you there?

Witness: I was on my way to work.

Plaintiff's Attorney: **Where** do you work?

Witness: At First National Bank, on Fifth Street.

Plaintiff's Attorney: **What** direction were you facing when you saw the accident?

Witness:	I was facing Main Street. Fifth and Main crossed Main Street to my right.
Plaintiff's Attorney:	**What**, if anything, was blocking your view?
Witness:	Nothing was blocking my view.
Plaintiff's Attorney:	**What** time was it when the accident occurred?
Witness:	About 10:00 a.m.
Plaintiff's Attorney:	Now, let's talk about the automobile collision you saw. **When** did you first see the plaintiff?
Witness:	I saw him when I got to the intersection.
Plaintiff's Attorney:	**Where** were you when you saw him?
Witness:	I was facing north, walking on Main Street.
Plaintiff's Attorney:	**What** direction was he traveling?
Witness:	From North to South, on Fifth Street.
Plaintiff's Attorney:	**When** did you first see the defendant?
Witness:	He was headed East on Main Street, about 200 feet from the intersection.
Plaintiff's Attorney:	**What** did you see next?
Witness:	The defendant was approaching the intersection and wasn't slowing down. He had the red light.
Plaintiff's Attorney:	**How** do you know he had the red light?
Witness:	I saw it because the cross-walk sign said I could walk, but he wasn't stopping. So, I looked carefully to see what color his light was.
Plaintiff's Attorney:	So, after you saw the defendant had the red light and saw him speeding toward the intersection, **what** happened next?
Witness:	The defendant kept coming toward the intersection and then finally slammed on his brakes, but it was too late. He ran into the plaintiff's car.
Plaintiff's Attorney:	**Where** was the plaintiff's car at the time the defendant him?
Witness:	In the middle of the intersection. He had the green light.

[You might have noticed that on one occasion in the sample, the questioner included the expression, "if anything," in the wording of the question. Some attorneys—and a few judges—believe that the inclusion of that wording automatically makes the question non-leading. That is an oversimplification. Suppose that a questioner asked, "**What** 2013 silver Ford Escape, if any, did you see enter the intersection?" In this question, the specific detail renders the question leading; it suggests that the car entering the intersection was a 2013 silver Ford Escape. Nevertheless, especially if the judge has just sustained a leading objection against you, it can be advisable to include "if anything" in the wording of the very next question. The inclusion of those words signals the judge that you understood his or her ruling and that you are making a bona fide effort to avoid leading.]

➢ CROSS EXAMINATION—R. 607–611

Evidence Casebook, pp. 73–78

[At common law, the elements of competency were perception, memory, narration, and sincerity. Even if the court does not read Rule 601 as abolishing the common-law competency requirements, in practice judges rarely rule that a witness is altogether incompetent. Rather, the judge allows the opposing attorney to expose the witness's deficiencies in these elements as a means of impeaching the witness's credibility. In general, a witness's credibility may be attacked by asking questions that relate to: (1) the witness's perception, (2) memory, (3) communication of the story, and (4) truthfulness. Notice that the following questions do not begin with natural interrogatory words. These questions are leading—often blatantly so. Rule 611(c)(1) expressly permits the use of leading questions on cross-examination. The use of leading phrasing is one of the cross-examiner's primary tools for maintaining control of opposing witnesses.]

(1) ***Perception.*** A witness's credibility may be undermined by casting doubt on the witness's ability to perceive what he claims to have witnessed. Assume in the following case that the defendant has been charged with stealing a briefcase from the victim.

Defense Attorney:	The person who stole your briefcase approached you from behind, didn't he?
Witness:	Yes.
Defense Attorney:	You were startled, weren't you, that a stranger grabbed your briefcase?
Witness:	Yes, that's true.
Defense Attorney:	It was after midnight when this theft that startled you took place, wasn't it?
Witness:	Yes.
Defense Attorney:	There wasn't a street light for at least three blocks in any direction, was there?

Witness:	No, there wasn't.
Defense Attorney:	After he ran up from behind you and suddenly grabbed the briefcase from your hand, he immediately began running away from you, correct?
Witness:	Yes.
Defense Attorney:	Isn't it true that as he ran away, you saw only the back of his head, not his face?
Witness:	Well, yes.
Defense Attorney:	So late one evening on a dark night, this person came up from behind you, abruptly snatched your briefcase, and then immediately ran away, so that you only saw his face, if at all, for only a split second, right?
Witness:	Yes. But . . .
Defense Attorney:	Thank you, no further questions.

[Consider the wording of the last question in the sample. Does it solicit any information that the witness has not already conceded? On one hand, it has the strategic effect of nicely summarizing the helpful concessions made by the witness; but, on the other hand, many judges would sustain the objection "asked and answered" or "cumulative" to that wording. It is true that while Rule 611(c) expressly governs leading questions, there is no explicit provision on cumulative questioning. However, Rule 611(a) gives the judge general discretionary control over the "mode" or form of the questioning. In the above example, a fair number of judges would have sustained an "asked and answered" objection to the last question. Although it can be a helpful summation of the concessions made by the witness, it can ruin the overall impression left by an otherwise effective line of cross-examination if you overreach at the end and conclude on a sustained objection.]

(2) ***Memory.*** If a witness has difficulty remembering an incident or a particular set of circumstances, that witness's credibility is called into question. Although the witness's recollection may be refreshed under Rule 612 [see next sample, infra], the very fact that a witness's recollection of events needs refreshing raises concern about the reliability of the testimony. The next illustration demonstrates an attack on the memory of a police officer witness in a drunk driving case.

Defense Attorney:	Officer, you arrested the defendant for suspicion of drunk driving nearly nine months ago, correct?
Witness/Officer:	Yes, that's correct.

Defense Attorney:	During the last nine months, you have made over two hundred traffic stops of drivers suspected of driving under the influence, right?
Witness:	That's about right.
Defense Attorney:	Now for each of those stops, about half of the time you conduct a field sobriety test, and the rest of the time you do not, is that right?
Witness:	Yes.
Defense Attorney:	You didn't write down whether you gave a test in this case, did you?
Witness:	No. It may not be in the report, but I remember I gave him a test.
Defense Attorney:	You also do not remember which type of test you supposedly gave, do you?
Witness:	No, it was some kind of field sobriety test though.
Defense Attorney:	Then it's your testimony that you don't remember what kind of test you gave him, isn't that correct?
Witness:	Well I suppose so.
Defense Attorney:	And isn't it true that you cannot tell us how my client performed on any such test because you can't tell us what kind of test it was?
Witness:	I just remember he failed whatever test I gave him.
Defense Attorney:	Thank you, no more questions.

[This is technically proper impeachment. However, when you conduct this type of questioning, it is important to adopt the appropriate demeanor. Do not become accusatory. Every juror knows that everyone forgets, and it can be counterproductive to adopt too aggressive a demeanor during this type of questioning. Juries connect much more naturally with witnesses and are often suspect of "tricky," overly aggressive attorneys. Elicit the concession of forgetfulness in a matter-of-fact manner. The concession gives you all the ammunition you need for closing argument. It would be an entirely different matter if you had "the goods" on the witness and could show that the witness is lying. That is not the case here.]

(3) ***Communication.*** Even if a witness has adequately perceived, and can sufficiently recall, events she may not be able to explain or effectively communicate them. In addition, a witness's "story" may not make sense, or may be contradictory, logically impossible, or

implausible. The following cross-examination is illustrative of how to impeach such a witness on cross-examination. Assume the defendant, Mr. Jones, is charged with illegally accessing child pornography on the internet. The prosecution has submitted authenticated computer records showing all the illegal child pornography websites visited by the defendant on his computer at work over a certain period of time and all e-mail activity of that computer for the same period.

Prosecutor:	Mr. Jones, you have admitted that your computer was used to access various child pornography web sites, isn't that right?
Defendant:	Yes, but someone set me up just to make me look bad.
Prosecutor:	Isn't it also true that the records contain the list of websites visited, the time of day those sites were visited, and all e-mail messages sent and received by your computer?
Defendant:	Yes, I can see that. Okay.
Prosecutor:	So, on January 23, 2014, at 1:01 p.m., the record shows that computer accessed, "Children Exposed," an illegal website, until 1:07 p.m. I read that correctly, didn't I?
Defendant:	Yes, you did.
Prosecutor:	And don't the records indicate that at 1:08 p.m., you sent an e-mail to your wife, Sally Jones?
Defendant:	That's what it says, yes.
Prosecutor:	And the substance of the e-mail was that you were telling her to call your mother?
Defendant:	Yes.
Prosecutor:	[That email you sent to your wife from your computer at 1:08 pm was sent just one minute after your computer had visited the "Children Exposed" illegal website, correct?
Defendant:	Yes.]
Prosecutor:	Isn't it true, Mr. Jones, that the very next entry on the computer record at 1:10 p.m.—within two minutes of your e-mail to your wife—is a search on Google for "naked pics of kids?"
Defendant:	Okay, alright, it says that, but you still can't prove it was me doing those searches.

Prosecutor:	But it was you who conducted these searches on your computer, wasn't it?
Defendant:	Look, I know it sounds crazy, but I think I remember leaving my office for something. I often do that at work, and then someone must have sneaked back into my office and used my computer.
Prosecutor:	Your secretary never [reported to you] seeing any strangers going into your office and then quickly leaving when you were not there, did she?
Defendant:	Well, then they must have had disguises, as janitors or something; plus, the people in the office are busy and maybe didn't notice.
Prosecutor:	No further questions.

[Notice that at the end of the line of questioning, the prosecutor does not ask the defendant how he "can expect" the jury to believe his last answer. It would be a mistake to do so. To begin with, there is no need to do so. The answer is so implausible that you have all the ammunition you need for closing argument. Moreover, under Rule 611(a) many judges would sustain the objection that the question would be "argumentative." The question would not seek any new substantive information from the witness; rather, it would merely challenge the witness about the plausibility of the answer. Again, you do not want to ruin an otherwise powerful line of questioning by ending on a sustained objection.]

(4) ***Veracity.*** A witness's truthfulness may be challenged by: (1) exposing a witness's personal or financial bias, giving the witness a reason to consciously lie or subconsciously distorting the witness's testimony; (2) confronting him with his own prior inconsistent statement, raising doubts about the truth of one or both statements; and (3) challenging his character for honesty, in effect demonstrating such an untruthful nature that the witness is not worthy of belief because he has a propensity to lie. The next example illustrates some of these attacks.

Defense Attorney:	Mr. White, let me see if I understand your testimony. Is it your testimony that my client, the defendant, hit the plaintiff after they had a collision in a parking lot?
Witness:	Yes.
Defense Attorney:	And you are testifying that afterwards, my client hit the plaintiff for no reason?
Witness:	Yeah, he sucker-punched him.
Defense Attorney:	Did you ever see the plaintiff hit my client?
Witness:	Yes, but only after your client hit first.

Defense Attorney:	After the collision, did a police officer arrive at the scene?
Witness:	Yes.
Defense Attorney:	In fact, an officer arrived within five minutes of the collision, right?
Witness:	I guess so.
Defense Attorney:	And didn't you tell that officer that the plaintiff hit my client first because he was angry about the defendant taking his parking place?
Witness:	Well, I may have said something like that, but I don't recall.
Defense Attorney:	The plaintiff is your brother-in-law, correct?
Witness:	Yes.
Defense Attorney:	And you live next door to the plaintiff and your sister, right?
Witness:	Yes.
Defense Attorney:	You are on very good terms with the plaintiff and your sister, aren't you?
Witness:	Yes.
Defense Attorney:	And isn't it true that you like to help the plaintiff out when you can?
Witness:	If I can.
Defense Attorney:	You would be pleased to see the plaintiff receive money for his injuries in this case, right?
Witness:	Of course. He deserves it.
Defense Attorney:	In fact, the plaintiff owes you over $10,000, doesn't he?
Witness:	I suppose.
Defense Attorney:	And the plaintiff hasn't even begun to pay you back, correct?
Witness:	That's ok, he's my brother-in-law. I know where he lives.
Defense Attorney:	You [might] receive some of your money back if the plaintiff wins this case, right?
Witness:	Maybe.

Defense Attorney:	Now, you would like this jury to believe your testimony in this case, isn't that right?[1]
Witness:	Of course I would. I'm telling the truth.

[This line of questioning raises questions about the witness's bias. Bias is one of the most popular impeachment techniques. In the first place, it is easy for lay jurors to understand the significance of bias Evidence. Moreover, when the witness has a bias, in closing you do not have to level the harsh accusation that due to the bias, the witness is committing perjury. Instead, in many cases you can argue that the bias may be influencing the witness's testimony at a subconscious level. The late Professor Irving Younger was one of the leading authorities on trial advocacy. He urged cross-examiners to use impeachment techniques that "go down easily." Subconscious influence is a much easier sell than outright perjury.]

➢ REFRESHED RECOLLECTION—R. 612

Evidence Casebook, pp. 83–74

How to Refresh a Witness's Memory

The following is an illustration of how the plaintiffs' lawyer in an employment hours lawsuit might have refreshed the witness's memory ("Mrs. Doty") under Rule 612:

Plaintiff's Attorney:	Mrs. Doty, how many hours did you work for Eddy Elias during the week of July 10th?
Mrs. Doty:	Well, I just don't remember. That was quite some time ago.
Plaintiff's Attorney:	Did you make a schedule listing the days and times you worked for Mr. Elias during the month of July?
Mrs. Doty:	Yes, I did.
Plaintiff's Attorney:	Would seeing that schedule now refresh your memory as to the number of hours you worked that week?
Mrs. Doty:	Yes, I think it would.
Plaintiff's Attorney:	May I approach the witness, your honor?
Judge:	Yes, you may.
Plaintiff's Attorney:	May the record reflect that I am showing Plaintiff's Exhibit 5 to opposing counsel for inspection?

[1] [This question is borderline argumentative, but some attorneys might chance it.]

Judge:	Any objections?
Defense Attorney:	No, Your Honor.
Plaintiff's Attorney:	I am now showing you Plaintiff's Exhibit 5. What is this document?
Mrs. Doty:	This is a listing of the hours I worked for Eddie during the month of July.
Plaintiff's Attorney:	Would you please read this document silently to yourself. When you are finished, place the document face down in front of you.
Mrs. Doty:	Yes, ok.
Plaintiff's Attorney:	Do you now remember how many hours you worked the week of July 10th for Mr. Elias?
Mrs. Doty:	Yes. I worked 45 hours that week.

[You can use Rule 612 on direct or cross-examination. It is especially important to know how to use Rule 612 on direct. In many cases, a witness is frightened at the prospect of testifying; that is especially true if the witness has never been to court before. Even when the witness confidently recalls everything during the pretrial conference at your office, he or she may become nervous when they enter the courtroom and see the robed judge, the armed bailiff, the attorneys, and all the other strangers in the room. Even well prepared, truthful witnesses often forget. However, if you can quickly and smoothly refresh their recollection, they can regain their composure and testify effectively. If you cannot do so, their demeanor may become more diffident and their testimony much less convincing. Moreover, during summation you can turn the witness's frank concession of forgetfulness to your advantage. What better proof of the witness's truthfulness? When the witness could not remember, the witness honestly and frankly conceded that.]

II. EXERCISE: DIRECT AND CROSS EXAMINATION

Part 1: Direct Examination. Assume you are the attorney for plaintiff, Nat Rogers (the neighbor who was harmed by the fire allegedly started by defendant Frank Derry), in the civil case (Appendix B). Prepare part of the direct examination of Nat Rogers with the goal of demonstrating that Frank Derry had a troubled relationship with his wife, Thelma. To that end, Nat had heard extreme fighting and anger at the Derry household, rumors of infidelity, and that Frank Derry said that he did not want to be responsible for any child support payments in the event of divorce. This would be used to show why Frank was motivated to harm his family by setting fire to his own house; which spread and caused major fire damages at Nat Roger's house. As you will see, it is important, and sometimes quite difficult, to ask simple, straightforward, unobjectionable questions during a direct examination, but just do your best at this point. Prepare and work with your witness and make sure to LISTEN to the witness's answers fully, and respond with any follow-up questions, if necessary, before moving on to your next question.

Part 2: Refreshed Recollection. Assume that during your direct examination of Nat Rogers (referenced above), he completely has forgotten: (1) how long his wife, Frederica, was receiving treatment at Nusquam State Hospital for her emotional trauma caused by the fire at their home; and (2) whether Federica was taking any medication at that time for her emotional trauma caused by the fire. Use the letter that Frederica wrote to Nat Rogers from the Nusquam State Hospital (Exhibit D, Chapter 10 [page 111]) as a writing used to refresh Nat Roger's recollection.

Part 3: Cross-Examination. Assume that Frank Derry has testified on his own behalf during the defendant's case-in-chief in the civil case. During his direct examination testimony, Frank Derry stated that he, "*has never been in any trouble with the law before.*" During your cross-examination of Frank Derry, use his Arrest and Conviction Record (Exhibit B, Chapter 10 [page108]) to impeach/attack the credibility of Frank Derry.

For All (3) Three Parts: During these three witness examinations, the rest of the class should just listen to the examination, and note any questions or objections they might have. When you are done questioning the witness, your professor can then critique your performance, as well as address any questions or objections raised by other members of the class. The important thing is to get on your feet, play the role of a lawyer, and try to elicit some important fact information from a witness that you would need to help prove your case.

CHAPTER 2

RELEVANCE

I. TIPS & POINTERS

Rule 401. Test for Relevant Evidence

Evidence is relevant if:

(a) it has a tendency to make a fact more or less probable than it would be without the evidence; and

(b) the fact is of consequence in determining the action.

Rule 402. General Admissibility of Relevant Evidence

Relevant evidence is admissible unless any of the following provides otherwise:

- the United States Constitution;
- a federal statute;
- these rules; or
- other rules prescribed by the Supreme Court.

Irrelevant evidence is not admissible.

At the base of every question of admissibility of evidence sits the concept of relevance. To the non-lawyer and the neophyte trial lawyer, the concept of relevance can be amorphous: "important," "related to the case," and "something that is essential to the proof" all are formulations that are sometimes bandied about. However, the definition under the Federal Rules is both specific and permissive.

As you see from the text of FRE 401, this definition of "relevance" has two parts: probativeness (also called "logical relevance") (subsection (a)) and materiality (sometimes called "legal relevance") (subsection (b)). For our practice exercises, keep in mind the following points about these components of the definition:

➢ The threshold for probativeness is very low. The offered evidence does not have to be *legally sufficient* to sustain the initial burden of production and "prove" the fact in question. It need not make the fact absolutely certain, "clear and convincing," proved "beyond a reasonable doubt" (the standard of proof in criminal cases), or even established by a preponderance of the evidence (the normal standard in civil cases). It suffices if it has "a tendency"—any tendency at all—to make the fact more or less probable. All it has to do is nudge the probability—a bit up or slightly down. The indefinite article, "a," shows the measure to be very small: good synonyms would be *scintilla, smidge, soupcon,* or *grain of sand.* Think of your case as a "brick wall." To be relevant, an item of evidence merely needs to be a "brick" in that wall.

- Look at this concept from the opposite perspective: given that the jury's function in a trial is to "weigh the disputed evidence," it follows that the evidence in question must at least have some "weight" to it, *i.e.*, some probativeness/logical relevance for the jury to weigh. If the evidence lacks any weight, it is inconsequential to the jury's determination of the verdict based on the weight of the evidence.

- In assessing probativeness, the court does not weigh the one piece of evidence against other pieces—that is, probativeness as an aspect of relevance is absolute, not relative. The question is not *how much* probative value the item has, but rather whether it has *any* value. Subject to other considerations of judicial efficiency (see discussion of Rule 403 in the next chapter), FRE 401 codifies a liberal approach to relevance.

- One of the most difficult aspects of Rule 401 for beginning lawyers to grasp is the point that the existence of competing, alternative inferences from a piece of evidence does not negate the "tendency" of the item to make a fact more or less likely. The court might agree with the opponent of the evidence that other inferences from the evidence are much more likely than that argued for by the profferor. Nevertheless, if the offered "tendency" is plausible—if it passes the "straight face" test—arguing the alternative inferences is left to the skill of the cross-examiner and the eloquence of her closing argument. (See, however, the discussion in the next chapter of the court's ability to regulate admissibility based on concerns of the "misleading" nature of the evidence under FRE 403.) Competing alternate inferences do not "cancel each other out" and render the evidence irrelevant. Instead, competing alternate inferences from an item of evidence mean that the evidence is relevant several ways on multiple theories, and the jury must decide which of the competing inferences to draw.

- The second leg of relevance, materiality, is generally tied to an analysis of the elements of the claims, charges, or defenses. Take, for example, the crime of possession of a firearm by a felon. In some jurisdictions, the crime requires proof of only two elements: (1) the defendant is a convicted felon, and (2) he possessed a firearm, *whether or not the firearm was in operating condition.* In such a jurisdiction, evidence concerning whether the firearm was operational cannot be material. In layman's terms, it does not matter if the firearm was in operating condition. Before the beginning of trial, read the relevant statutes and anticipated jury instructions and key your relevance arguments to the legal elements set out in those instructions, which define the essential elements of the claims, charges, and defenses. As a further example, if the charged offense is a general mens rea crime, the defense cannot introduce evidence of the defendant's voluntary intoxication to negate the mens rea.

II. EXERCISE: PRE-TRIAL MOTION ("IN LIMINE") TO EXCLUDE EVIDENCE AS IRRELEVANT

Part 1: Memorandum of Law. You are an Assistant District Attorney on the team preparing the prosecution of Frank Derry in the criminal case (Appendix A). The Chief DA has asked you to prepare a memorandum opposing defendant's pre-trial motion (also called a "motion in limine [on the threshold]") seeking to have the court exclude, in advance of the opening of trial, certain items of evidence the prosecution plans to offer. The Chief DA tells you that while the defense probably realizes their chances of complete success are slim given the permissive definition of relevance in FRE 401, the clever defense lawyer may be hoping to persuade the court that the prosecution is "grasping at straws" in relying on relatively weak items of evidence. In other words, the defense attorney wants to bias the judge against the prosecution even before the prosecution calls its first witness. An early, negative view of the prosecution case could lead the judge to view mid-trial issues more favorably to the defense. For that reason, your boss wants to make an aggressive response justifying the admission of these items of evidence. Your marching orders are to make the strongest arguments that the items pass the test of relevance under Rule 401.

Draft and submit a Memorandum of Law not to exceed two pages in length, double-spaced, opposing the defense's motion to exclude the following items of evidence. In essence, the defense has argued that each item has no tendency at all to make any fact of consequence to the case more or less likely that it would be without the item. You may *not* cite cases, but must ground your arguments solely on the text of Rule 401 and any supporting language in the Advisory Committee Notes.[1] This is the Age of Statutes, and the starting point for your argument ought to be the language of the Rule.

- *Item 1*: Frank Derry and his wife Thelma had their first child before they were married, at ages 18 and 16, respectively.
- *Item 2*: Derry did not graduate from high school. He is employed as a Senior Mechanic at the local Ford dealership, where he has reached the top of the pay scale for non-high school graduates, at $28,000/year.

[1] The authors acknowledge that this restriction is unrealistic; no memorandum of law in actual practice would omit supporting case law. However, the goal of these exercises is to develop the skill to argue effectively within the rules of evidence; they are not intended to replace, or even to supplement, legal research and writing training. To be feasible within the confines of a podium Evidence course, we must hold the writing requirements to a minimum. It is important to see that in addition to lawyers reacting verbally to objections during trial or depositions, lawyers often will write their arguments in Motion in Limine briefs.

- *Item 3*: Neighbors of the Derrys are prepared to testify that they often hear loud, heated arguments between the couple, often late at night. According to these witnesses, more often than not the subject of the arguments appeared to be the couple's finances.

Part 2: Oral Argument on the Motion. Assume the judge has called for a hearing on the motion in limine in order to ask questions and hear oral argument about the legal issues raised in the motion. One or more participants will be assigned to argue the prosecution side of the motion in class. One or more participants will be assigned to counter with the defense's best arguments to show why these items of evidence are not relevant. One or more participants will be assigned the role of the judge to hear the motion and to question the attorneys concerning their positions.

CHAPTER 3

403

I. TIPS & POINTERS

> **Rule 403. Excluding Relevant Evidence for Prejudice, Confusion, Waste of Time, or Other Reasons**
>
> The court may exclude relevant evidence if its probative value is substantially outweighed by a danger of one or more of the following: unfair prejudice, confusing the issues, misleading the jury, undue delay, wasting time, or needlessly presenting cumulative evidence.

Once we grasp the concepts that all relevant evidence is generally admissible and the threshold of relevance is very low, we immediately confront a set of rules declaring certain kinds of evidence "relevant but inadmissible." FRE 403 through 415 address these types of evidence. In some cases, the exclusion is due to social policy considerations. For instance, statements made by the defendant in criminal plea discussions are ordinarily not admissible. The importance of plea agreements in streamlining an overburdened criminal justice system trumps the probative value of what the defendant said; therefore, FRE 410 protects the defendant's ability to speak freely during such negotiations. FRE 410's exclusionary rule reduces the defendant's fear that any candid statements he or she makes during pretrial plea bargaining will come back to haunt the defense at trial.

FRE 403 is perhaps the most used of all the "relevant but inadmissible" rules. It gives the court wide discretion to regulate what evidence is admitted or excluded—much wider latitude than many other rules of inadmissibility. (See, *e.g.*, the chapters *infra* on FRE 404 (character) and FRE 801 (hearsay).) Clearly, then, it is important to have a working knowledge of Rule 403 in one's arsenal as a trial lawyer. Its proper use requires understanding not only the language of the rule, but also these points:

- The rule does not prevent "prejudice" pure and simple. The statute refers to "unfair" prejudice. Your opponent's evidence is *supposed* to hurt your case—either by damaging your proof or by supporting her proof—if it did not do so, then it would not be relevant evidence. That kind of "prejudice" is what trials are all about. If you understand that, you will never make the foolish argument that the evidence should be excluded because, in essence, "it's killing us, Your Honor." If you say that, after snickering the judge and your opponent will immediately know that your grasp of evidence law is tenuous. Instead, explain how the evidence's prejudice is "*unfair*." The rule is not designed to keep the trial close, only "fair."

> Imagine a double murder case. The prosecutor wants to prove how and where the victims' bodies were situated when they were found, by introducing gruesome crime-scene photographs of the bloody and bludgeoned bodies *in situ*. Although this evidence is certainly relevant, the nature of the photographs may shock the jury to such an extent that the jurors will want to convict somebody—maybe even anybody—based on passion or sympathy for the victims and their families. Thus the risk is that the jury's deliberations concerning the defendant's guilt or innocence may be distorted by emotional bias and outrage.

- "FRE 403 encompasses two analytically distinct but frequently overlapping forms of unfair prejudice. The first is the injection of undue emotionalism into the proceeding arousing hostility, anger, or sympathy on the part of the jury. [See example *supra*.] The second is the likelihood that the jury will misuse the evidence in some way or give it undue weight."[1] Either type of prejudice creates the risk that the jury will decide the case on an improper basis. The judge realizes that technically, the item of evidence is logically relevant under FRE 401. However, drawing on his or her knowledge of juror psychology, the judge believes that realistically, the admission of the evidence will tempt the jury to decide the case on an impermissible basis.

- When arguing a 403 issue, remember that it involves *balancing* probative value (the probativeness half of Rule 401) against unfair prejudice. Always address *both sides* of the balancing scales. If you are opposing the evidence, stress not only the amount of unfair prejudice (tying it, of course, to the danger of either emotionalism or improper reasoning), but also the minimal amount of probative value. Conversely, if you are offering the evidence and opposing the 403 objection, in your argument elaborate on the quantum of probative value and diminish the danger of unfair prejudice.

> For example, in the double-murder hypothetical *supra*, the prosecutor might argue in favor of admissibility as follows: "The position of the bodies—both their proximity to each other and the obviously turbulent nature of the struggle that caused the awkward, twisted way in which they both fell—will greatly assist the jury's assessment of the likelihood that both deaths were caused by one person and with great violence. As to the danger of the jury's reacting emotionally—

---

1 Mueller & Kirkpatrick, *Evidence* § 4.10 at 175 (4th ed. 2009), citing *United States v. Pintado-Isiordia*, 448 F.3d 1155 (9th Cir. 2006) (only purpose for photograph of defendant in military uniform, when his service was shown by other evidence, was "to elicit jury's sympathy and patriotism"); *United States v. Looking Cloud*, 419 F.3d 781 (8th Cir. 2005) (evidence is unfairly prejudicial if it encourages jury to find guilt on basis of "improper reasoning").

they can see this kind of image at the movies and on television daily. We can safely assume that the jurors have not led such sheltered lives that they will react with emotionalism that would distort their reasoning."

- The text of the statute declares that the judge must find that the danger of unfair prejudice *substantially outweighs* the probative value. In other words, Rule 403 clearly favors *ad*missibility over *inad*missibility. Other rules of inclusion/exclusion—*e.g.,* 404, 407–415, and 608–609 concerning impeachment of witnesses—are tilted more towards exclusion. Therefore, if you are the opponent, it is advisable to cite more specific exclusionary rules, such as hearsay, before invoking 403. The more specific rules constrain the judge's discretion to a greater degree than Rule 403, and so objections based on them are more likely to succeed.

- Consider having a "Plan B." If it looks likely the evidence will be admitted, consider *stipulating* to the fact the proponent is offering the evidence to prove. "Defense will stipulate that the murder was violent and to the positioning of the bodies so that the photos need not be shown." Your stipulation can eliminate any legitimate need for the proponent to resort to the unfairly prejudicial evidence. Conversely, if it looks like the evidence will be excluded, consider asking the judge to admit it with a *limiting instruction* that will minimize the prejudice: "The jury will disregard the gruesome aspects of the photos and consider the photos only to show the violence of the deaths and the positioning of the bodies." (Reasonable minds differ over the effectiveness of such an instruction—can the jury really follow it and do what they are directed? Moreover, there is a risk that the instruction will serve only to emphasize the prejudicial evidence. Re-read the instruction we just used as an example, in which the judge intones ". . . gruesome aspects . . . violence of the deaths. . . ." Do you want the jury to hear this from the judge?)

- While the danger of unfair prejudice is the most frequently used component of Rule 403 for excluding evidence, do not ignore the Rule's other bases for exclusion: "confusion of the issues" (which analytically may be roughly the same as "unfair prejudice" in its second meaning of improper reasoning), "misleading the jury" (another similar consideration), "undue delay, waste of time, or needless presentation of cumulative evidence." Time consumption—mentioned three times in the Rule!—is persuasive to many judges, for whom time is a very precious commodity. Often it helps, as the opponent, to combine several factors.

    The opponent of the photographs in the double-murder case, *supra,* might argue: "In addition to the grave danger that the jury will react emotionally to these graphic photographs, we urge Your Honor to consider that there is other, readily available, less prejudicial evidence of the facts the prosecution offering the photographs to prove. The forensic team drew a precise diagram showing the proximity of the bodies. As to the 'awkward, twisted' postures cited by prosecution, the use of bendable mannequins could supply that detail in a less alarming way. And of course, the investigating detective's description of how he found the bodies and how they appeared to him at the time—which he could supplement with an in-court drawing—will supply other details. In short, the prosecution has no legitimate need to resort to these gruesome photos. They should be excluded as needlessly cumulative."

- Finally, note the qualifier "needlessly" modifying "cumulative evidence." The presentation of cumulative evidence is a large part of what is supposed to happen at trial. We pile up the evidence on our side to reinforce its persuasive power. We ask several witnesses to recite the same facts to corroborate one another. It is only when it seems like "enough, already" that the judge will sustain a Rule 403 objection based on cumulativeness. Seasoned trial lawyers watch for the judge's clues—rolling the eyes, nervous shifting in the seat, heavy sighs, a question to the examining lawyer along the lines of "How much more do you have on this, counsel?" or eyes closed/sounds of snoring—to identify the point at which the judge has reached her limit. If as the proponent of the evidence you want to defeat the objection, emphasize that you are offering the corroborative evidence on a "central issue in the case." You need "cumulative" evidence on such issues.

II. EXERCISE: TRIAL IN PROGRESS—PREPARE TO OPPOSE/DEFEND ADMISSIBILITY OF EVIDENCE

In plaintiff's case-in-chief in the civil trial, *Rogers v. Derry,* plaintiff Rogers is testifying. After he has described his personal background (education, occupation, length of time he has lived next-door to Derry), his counsel starts the following line of questioning. One-half of the class will be appointed in advance of class time to be prepared to argue plaintiff's side of the issue, one-half defendant's. In class, the professor will announce which students will actually stand and make arguments. She will also appoint one or more students to play the judge and rule on the objections. Before class, review this entire transcript and pre-prepare your objections (for defendant), your defense of the admissibility of the evidence (for plaintiff) and your supporting arguments. In this simulation, the only rules you need to cite are 401, 402, and 403. As the Introduction noted, do not be content to cite or paraphrase the relevant rule. Rather, be ready to directly quote the specific statutory language you are relying on. Show the judge that you have the better command of the governing statutes. As Felix Frankfurter famously said, "Read the statute. Read the statute. And read the statute."

NAT ROGERS et ux., Plaintiffs	:	Novurbana Superior Court
v.	:	Civil Docket
FRANK DERRY, Defendant	:	No. 103 CIV YR-1

TRIAL TRANSCRIPT—DAY 2

DIRECT EXAMINATION OF NAT ROGERS, continued:

Q Yesterday we finished your testimony concerning the fact that, before the fire, you and Mr. Derry had been neighbors for three years. In that period of time, what social contact, if any, did you and Derry have?

A Nothing much beyond saying hello when we saw each other in our driveways or cutting our grass. Except I have to say, Derry was never out there much cutting his grass—he let it get pretty long. Made a bit of an eyesore to the neighborhood, and made me worry about my property value with what you might call a "slum" next door.

Q Beyond those brief contacts, did you and Derry ever socialize?

A No. My wife and I invited them over to our holiday open house each December, but they only came once—the first year. Ms. Derry got pretty drunk pretty quick on my wife's eggnog, so they left early. Derry had to hold her up so she could make it home to next door, she was staggering so bad. We still invited them the next two years, but they didn't come. In fact, they didn't even have the courtesy to RSVP.

Q Do you have any information about the Derrys' home life?

A Yes, I do. Our housing development has really tight lot lines, and the floor plans are mirror images from one house to the next. So our kitchen wall is only a few feet from their kitchen wall. That means we can hear a lot of what goes on in their house.

Q What has that told you about their home life?

A They have lots of loud arguments—like screaming at each other.

Q What are these arguments about?

A A lot of them seem to be about money. He shouts at her that she's spending too much. She shouts at him that he should be making more money. And a lot of the time during these arguments, I hear the kids crying.

Q Over what duration, during the three years you were neighbors before the fire, did these arguments occur?

A Well, I heard them ever since they moved in back in October YR-5, but it seems like they got more frequent in the last year, that is, YR-2. At the beginning I would say they happened every few weeks, but in YR-2 it seemed like they were happening about twice a week.

Q Did you notice any change in the subject matter of the arguments during YR-2?

A They mentioned money more and more. And a lot of times I heard Ms. Derry use the word "divorce." I noticed that especially in the Fall months of YR-2—it seemed like things were really heating up between them.

[A brief recess is called while the Court takes a guilty plea in an unrelated matter.]

Q Mr. Rogers, we're going to get to the issue of how the fire happened a bit later. First, though, I want to ask you about what damages you feel you have suffered as a result. What are the components of your damages claims?

A Of course, we lost our house and the value of it and its contents. But what feels even worse is the wreck it has made of our lives emotionally. I consider myself a pretty strong person emotionally, but recovering from this fire has been really tough. It's been even worse for my wife, let me tell you.

Q What are the effects you have seen on her?

A It started the day after the fire. When the Fire Department told us it was safe to go back there and see what we could find in the rubble—in case there was anything left that could be salvaged from our personal possessions—we drove up and Freddie (that's my nickname for her, my wife Frederica) burst into tears as soon as she saw the wreckage.

Q What happened next?

A We started picking our way through the ashes, and when we got to the kitchen Freddie fell down to her knees and started sobbing uncontrollably. She started wailing, "This is where I fed our babies their first little jars of Gerbers peaches . . . this is where the high chair was . . . this is where they sat crayoning . . . remember how Zelda tried to stay between the lines but Zack said he 'didn't care about no lines'?" Poor Freddie was so upset, I almost thought I was going to have to call an ambulance.

Q How are you able to remember all this in such detail?

A I was videotaping to record the physical damage to the house. When I heard Freddie wailing in the kitchen, I went over and got it all on tape. I brought the tape with me to court today.

Q Your Honor, at this time we request permission to play the videotape to the jury.

[Assume, for timing purposes, that, if allowed, the showing of the tape takes the trial through to the lunch recess. Upon return after lunch, Rogers's direct examination resumes:]

Q What other evidence do you have to support your claims for emotional distress to you or your wife?

A To show you how scary and violent the fire was, it will tell you a lot if you know how badly Ms. Derry and their kids were burned.

A Your Honor, these eight photographs, pre-marked as P-7 through P-15 for Identification, have been stipulated by defense to be authentic photos of Ms. Derry and the three Derry children at the hospital two days after the fire. We move them into evidence.

[The eight photographs appear below and on the next pages.]

Ex. P-7 for Identification

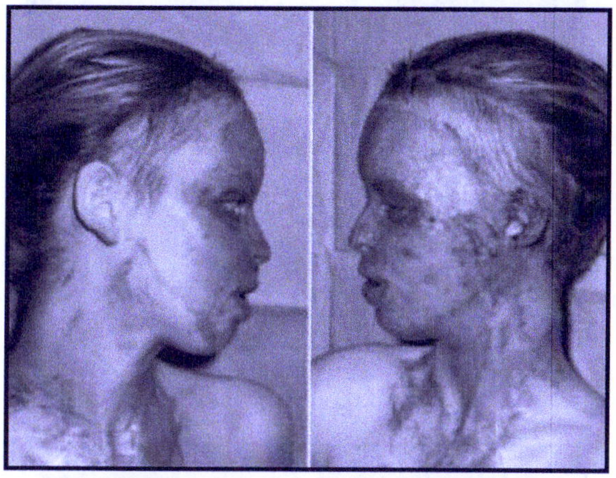

Ex. P-8 for Identification

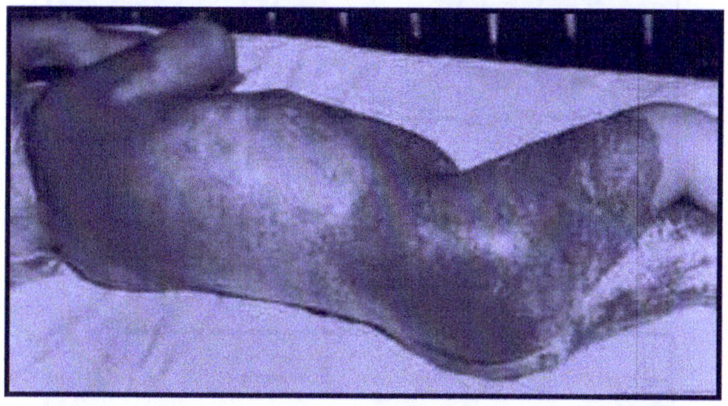

Ex. P-9 for Identification

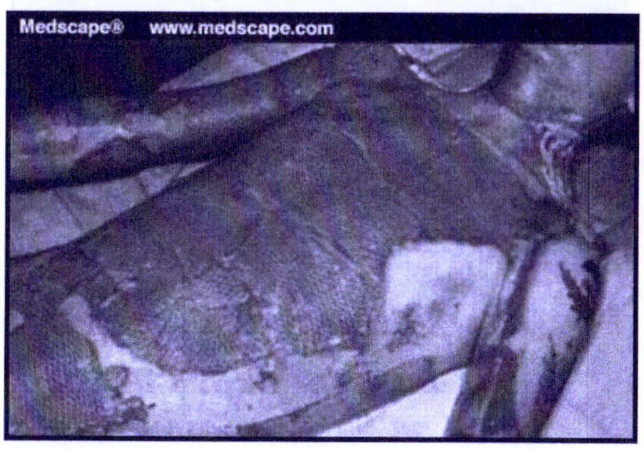

Ex. P-10 for Identification

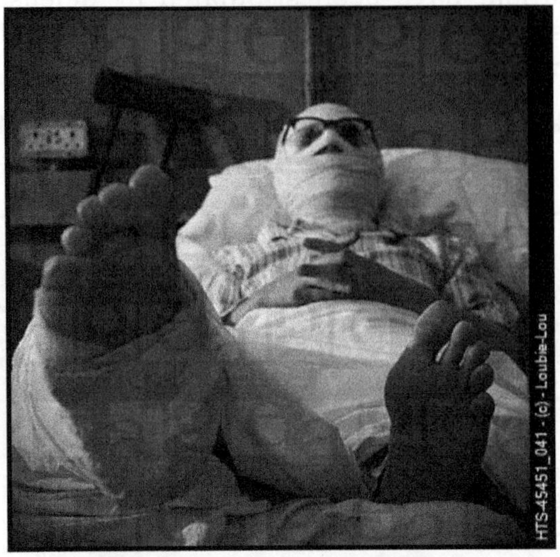

Ex. P-11 for Identification

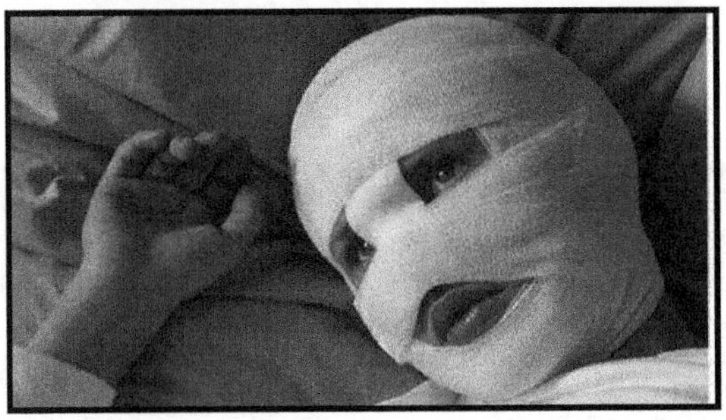

Ex. P-12 for Identification

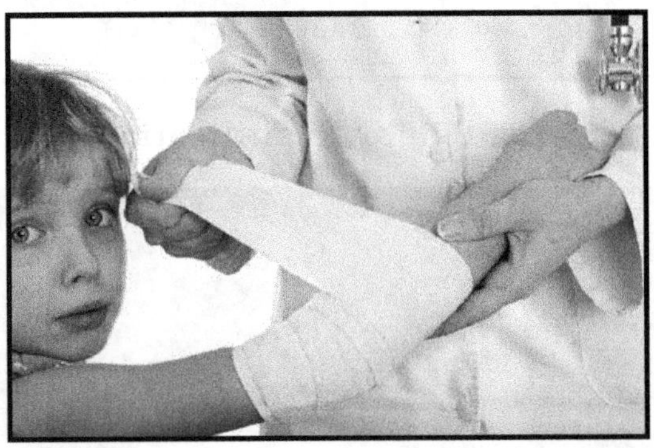

Ex. P-13 for Identification

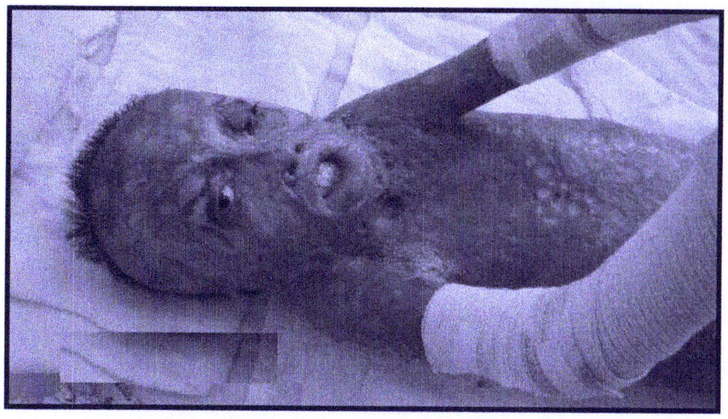

Ex. P-14 for Identification

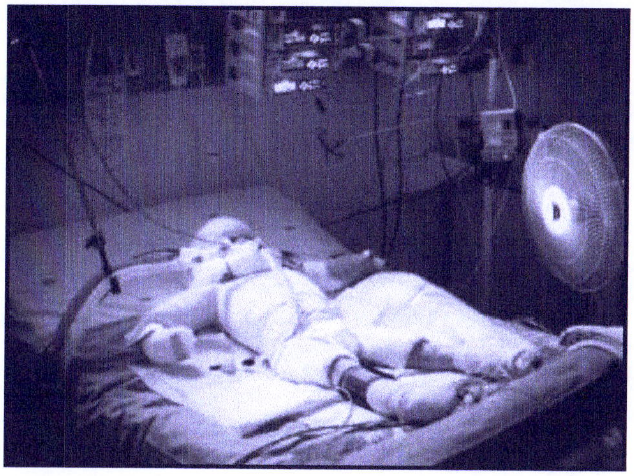

[End of Exercise]

CHAPTER 4

CHARACTER

I. TIPS & POINTERS

Rule 404. Character Evidence; Crimes or Other Acts

(a) Character Evidence.

(1) ***Prohibited Uses.*** Evidence of a person's character or character trait is not admissible to prove that on a particular occasion the person acted in accordance with the character or trait.

(2) ***Exceptions for a Defendant or Victim in a Criminal Case.*** The following exceptions apply in a criminal case:

(A) a defendant may offer evidence of the defendant's pertinent trait, and if the evidence is admitted, the prosecutor may offer evidence to rebut it;

(B) subject to the limitations in Rule 412, a defendant may offer evidence of an alleged victim's pertinent trait, and if the evidence is admitted, the prosecutor may:

(i) offer evidence to rebut it; and

(ii) offer evidence of the defendant's same trait; and

(C) in a homicide case, the prosecutor may offer evidence of the alleged victim's trait of peacefulness to rebut evidence that the victim was the first aggressor.

(3) ***Exceptions for a Witness.*** Evidence of a witness's character may be admitted under Rules 607, 608, and 609.

(b) Crimes, Wrongs, or Other Acts.

(1) ***Prohibited Uses.*** Evidence of a crime, wrong, or other act is not admissible to prove a person's character in order to show that on a particular occasion the person acted in accordance with the character.

(2) ***Permitted Uses; Notice in a Criminal Case.*** This evidence may be admissible for another purpose, such as proving motive, opportunity, intent, preparation, plan, knowledge, identity, absence of mistake, or lack of accident. On request by a defendant in a criminal case, the prosecutor must:

(A) provide reasonable notice of the general nature of any such evidence that the prosecutor intends to offer at trial; and

(B) do so before trial—or during trial if the court, for good cause, excuses lack of pretrial notice.

Rule 405. Methods of Proving Character

(a) By Reputation or Opinion. When evidence of a person's character or character trait is admissible, it may be proved by testimony about the person's reputation or by testimony in the form of an opinion. On cross-examination of the character witness, the court may allow an inquiry into relevant specific instances of the person's conduct.

(b) By Specific Instances of Conduct. When a person's character or character trait is an essential element of a charge, claim, or defense, the character or trait may also be proved by relevant specific instances of the person's conduct.

There is probably no subject of evidence law more perplexing than character evidence. In part this is due to the difficulty in defining "character." Further, FRE 404–405, which regulate the subject, are awkwardly phrased. Yet, because they have been the foundation of rulings on the subject since the adoption of the Federal Rules in the mid-1970s, there has been a reluctance to rewrite them substantially. Even in the 2011 "re-styling" of FRE, for example, only modest changes were made.

The difficulty of character evidence for many students may lay in the fact that from a lay perspective, such evidence seems highly probative. In everyday life, we routinely rely on character reasoning such as inferences based on stereotypes. Hence, it would seem to follow that a great deal of character evidence should be admissible, especially in light of the Rules' preference for admissibility. Yet what students discover is that very little character evidence ever comes in at trial. Of course, this surprises them.

We will address these difficulties from several angles.

- Here is one definition of "character": "As used in the Rules, "character" means a person's disposition or propensity to engage, or not to engage, in various forms of conduct. Viewed from this perspective, character is not a unitary concept. Everyone has multiple traits of character that may include a propensity to be truthful (or dishonest), drive safely (or recklessly), drink temperately (or excessively or not at all), or act peaceably (or violently)." Mueller & Kirkpatrick, *Evidence* § 4.11 (4th ed. 2009). In plainer words, whenever the evidence is offered to show what an actor in the lawsuit's underlying facts "is like," or "how he acted" on another occasion, you should question whether the actor's "character" is being offered. When the proponent relies on a "character" theory of logical relevance, the proponent is ordinarily using the character or character trait as circumstantial proof of conduct, *i.e.*, he is suggesting that the reputation, opinion, or act shows that the person has a character trait, and in turn this increases the probability that the person acted consistently with that trait on the occasion in question.

- It will help to distinguish between *character as substantive evidence* on the historical merits to prove that something did (or did not) happen in the case, and *character for impeachment* to show that a witness did (or did not) lie during his testimony. In this chapter, we will address substantive use, usually of a criminal defendant or a criminal victim, and defer impeachment use—that the witness has bad character for truthfulness—to Chapter 5. In that chapter, we encounter one of the great inconsistencies in Evidence law—the sharp contrast between the general permissibility of character reasoning related to credibility and the severe restrictions on character reasoning related to the historical merits. Within substantive use on the merits, we can distinguish between *direct use* (where character is an essential element of a claim, charge, or defense—Rule 405(b)) and the far more common *circumstantial use* (where character is used to suggest that an actor's character trait, or his behavior on occasions other than those in the facts of the case, makes it more likely that he behaved in a similar way in the case). That theory is commonly referred to as "propensity" evidence—again, character used as circumstantial proof of conduct.

- *Situations in which character is* ***DIRECTLY IN ISSUE.*** Taking direct use first: In simplest terms, FRE 405(b) allows specific instances to prove character when character itself is an issue in the case. Moreover, under FRE 402 all relevant evidence is admissible unless barred by a rule. Given 402, students might think that character-in-issue evidence would produce a good deal of admissible character evidence. But in fact, the number of claims, charges, or defenses that include character as an essential element is very small. These are rare cases in which the substantive law requires an allegation of a character trait—not mere conduct—in the pleadings. Your professor will go over these with you in your studies. The two most common examples from civil practice and the one from the criminal side illustrate the narrowness of the field.

  - In a civil action for child custody, the character of the parents is an essential element in the court's consideration of the child's best interests. The central issue is the person's fitness as a parent.

  - In a civil action for negligent entrustment of responsibility (*e.g.*, to a person employed as a bar bouncer) or negligent supervision (*e.g.*, of a train engineer who has a history of drunkenness on the job), the character of the person entrusted or supervised is an element of the plaintiff's proof of the defendant's alleged negligence.[1]

[1] Compare a claim based on *respondeat superior*, where the employer's knowledge of the employee's character, and indeed the employee's character itself, are irrelevant, because the employer is vicariously liable for the employee's job-related actions. In contrast, when the plaintiff

- In a criminal case in which the defendant contends he was entrapped into committing the crime alleged, the defendant's character—his "predisposition" or lack of same to commit the crime—is an element the fact-finder must consider in determining whether he was entrapped.
- When character is directly in issue, the parties may use all three methods of proving character—reputation, opinion, and specific acts.

➢ *Situations in which character is used as **CIRCUMSTANTIAL PROOF OF CONDUCT.*** As to circumstantial use on the historical merits, FRE 404–405 bar general propensity evidence except in limited situations. To generalize, we are not permitted to reason that because an actor has "done it before" on another occasion, it is more likely he "did it again in this case." Your studies and readings will have elucidated the reasons for evidence law's reluctance to allow propensity evidence. Here it suffices to make two points. First, this antipathy to propensity evidence is counter-intuitive, as most lay people think that an actor's conduct on other occasions is a sound basis for drawing inferences about his conduct in the case at trial. Second, in our experience students fare best with the issue if they accept the general ban as a given and concentrate on learning to recognize the handful of exceptions: FRE 404(a)(2)(A) concerning a criminal defendant's character, FRE 404(a)(2)(B) relating to a criminal victim's character and the defendant's "same trait", FRE 404(a)(2)(C) concerning a criminal victim's character in a homicide case, FRE 404(a)(3) governing impeachment use of character, and the provisions in FRE 413–15 for sexual assault and child molestation cases

Assuming that one of these exceptions applies and allows you to use character as circumstantial proof of conduct, what methods of proof may you use? Here character may ordinarily be proved only by reputation and/or opinion, not by extrinsic evidence of a specific instance of conduct. (A specific instance of conduct can be inquired about on cross-examination of a character witness, if there is a good-faith basis in fact for the question. The theory is that the inquiry is relevant to show the witness's credibility, not the defendant's character. If the witness claimed to be familiar with the person's reputation for peacefulness but had not heard that the person had recently been indicted for murder, the reliability of the reputation testimony is questionable. But the attorney is stuck with whatever answer the character witness provides.) The impeachment character rules, FRE 608–609, and the sex offense

claims negligent entrustment or supervision, the plaintiff is alleging personal fault on the part of the employer. An advantage of a claim based on negligent supervision is the availability of punitive damages.

and child molestation rules, FRE 412–415, contain their own exceptional methods-of-proof provisions.

- *Situations in which evidence of a specific act is relevant on* ***A NON-CHARACTER THEORY OF LOGICAL RELEVANCE.*** When the proponent invokes this theory, the proponent must offer testimony about a specific act, not reputation or opinion. Once you have internalized that the use of propensity evidence as circumstantial proof of conduct is generally forbidden and that its permitted uses are limited to the criminal defendant's pertinent character, the criminal victim's pertinent character, and impeachment of witnesses, you must learn to spot the so-called "non-character" uses allowed by FRE 404(b)(2): motive, intent, absence of mistake or accident, identity, common plan or scheme, opportunity, and preparation/plan/knowledge. (The mnemonic **M-I-A-M-I C-O-P** can help you recall this list.) Often these "non-character uses" sound a lot like propensity evidence in disguise. Indeed, some respected commentators believe that they boil down to propensity evidence masquerading as non-character evidence. However, the law is settled that these "other purposes" listed in 404(b)(2) (and similar uses, since the non-exclusive list is prefaced by "such as") are allowable "non-character" uses of the actor's specific act. Technically, these theories of logical relevance do not include any intermediate inference as to the person's propensity or character. When the judge admits the evidence, on request the judge gives the jury a Rule 105 limiting instruction that (a) specifies the legitimate use of the evidence and (b) forbids the jury from treating the testimony as evidence of the person's character. Rule 404(b)(2) is of huge importance in criminal cases. It generates more published opinions than any other provision of the FRE. In civil cases plaintiffs are increasingly using Rule 404(b)(2) to justify the admission of other misconduct to prove entitlement to punitive damages.

  Recall our discussion of the available Rule 403 objection of "needlessly cumulative" in Chapter 2. That objection could come into play in a Rule 404(b) situation. A judge might be persuaded to bar evidence of another act offered to prove "another purpose" under Rule 404(b) because of the need for a "trial within a trial." The defense counsel might tell the judge that if the judge admits the evidence of the other alleged act, the defense will be compelled to establish the defendant's "alibi" for the uncharged act. "If Your Honor allows this diversion, the prosecutor will have to call at least three additional witnesses to attempt to prove the prosecution's facts, followed by our two alibi witnesses—a trial within a trial." This is a good illustration of the interrelationship of the rules.

II. EXERCISE: TRIAL IN PROGRESS—PREPARE TO OPPOSE/DEFEND ADMISSIBILITY OF EVIDENCE

The criminal case, *State v. Derry*, is at trial. Your instructor will appoint prosecutors, defenders, and judges to act out the following portions of the trial. All students should prepare in advance to make arguments in support of and in opposition to the offered testimony insofar as it seeks to offer character evidence. NOTE: pay particular attention to the phase of trial in which the portion of testimony is being offered, as this will affect your analysis under FRE 404(a).

STATE OF NUSQUAM	:	Novurbana Superior Court
v.	:	Criminal Docket
FRANK DERRY, Defendant	:	No. 2,065 CRIM YR-2

TRIAL TRANSCRIPT—DAY 2

In the Prosecution's case-in-chief:

DIRECT EXAMINATION OF NAT ROGERS, continued:

Q Yesterday we finished your testimony concerning the fact that, before the fire, you and Mr. Derry had been neighbors for three years. In that period of time, what social contact, if any, did you and Derry have?

A Nothing much beyond saying hello when we saw each other in our driveways or cutting our grass. Except I have to say, Derry was never out there much cutting his grass—he let it get pretty long. I complained to him about it several times in the first year after they moved in. Each time, he told me, "I cut it last weekend—it just grows really fast." But each time I had been home on those weekends, and he hadn't cut it—so he was trying to get out of it with an obvious lie.

Q Beyond those brief contacts, did you and Derry ever socialize?

A No. My wife and I invited them over to our holiday open house each December, but they only came once—the first year. Ms. Derry got pretty drunk pretty quick on my wife's eggnog, so they left early. Derry had to hold her up so she could make it home to next door, she was staggering so bad. But I gotta tell you, Frank was even drunker than she was—but I guess he was used to drinking a lot, because he could still walk better than she could. He was slurring his words so bad you couldn't tell he was speaking English!

Q Do you know any of the people Mr. Derry associates with around town?

A Yeah. We both belong to the Little League Boosters Club. It raises money for the boys' Little League and the girls' Slo-Pitch League. Our kids and the Derrys' kids are in those. So we and the Derrys attend the same organizational meetings and fund-raisers, and also about twice a year we have a Club Dinner to give out playing awards to the kids and service awards to the parents who did the most for the Club.

Q What can you tell us about Frank Derry's involvement in the Club?

A Even though he's been coming to it ever since they moved in, he doesn't do anything that I have seen. He comes to most of the meetings—doesn't say anything—doesn't seem to have any suggestions or new ideas—and I've never heard him volunteer to do anything or take on any jobs. It always looks to me like he's there for the free food and beer, and to check out the ladies in attendance. He does seem to have a "roving eye."

Q Beyond his "eye roving," have you seen anything to back up your feeling that he is "checking out the ladies"?

A One meeting in the summer of the year of the fire, I was standing near him while he was talking to one of the moms—a divorced lady who was pretty good-looking—and I heard him say to her, "Here's my cell number—call me if you want to grab a coffee sometime." She said, "What would your wife say?" He said back, "You let me worry about her. If you want the coffee, I've got the time."

Q Are you aware of any reputation Frank Derry has among the members of the Club?

A Yes, he has the reputation of being untrustworthy—like he says he'll do stuff but then he doesn't.

Q How about his personality, particularly anything having to do with violence?

A I've heard a bunch of members say a bunch of times, "Don't push him very hard to get him to do stuff. He's got a hair-trigger temper and when he blows up, he gets pretty violent."

Q Now how about yourself, Mr. Rogers. Have you had any experience with Mr. Derry that gives you an opinion whether he's prone to violence?

A Yes, I have some encounters that give me an opinion on that.

Q Without going into the details, generally describe the situation and tell us your opinion.

A I told you already about my getting on him for letting his grass grow long and make the neighborhood look bad. In the year before the fire those discussions got pretty heated, and I got the impression Frank was pretty hot under the collar. Made me decide to cool it on the subject—I didn't want him to get physical with me.

Q To your recollection, did you do anything that you thought would have provoked that kind of reaction from Mr. Derry?

A Heck, no, I'm about the most peaceful, non-violent person you could hope to meet. I keep cool and try real hard not to be "in your face" to anybody. In fact, I'm proud to say I have never had a physical fight in my life, and I almost never get into arguments either. I use "Friendly Persuasion," like my Quaker Daddy used to say when he was raising us.

[Rogers's testimony continues on other subjects; end of excerpt for this exercise.]

* * * * *

TRIAL TRANSCRIPT—DAY 5

In the Defense case [the Defense calls its first witness]:

DIRECT EXAMINATION OF EDWARD DERRY:

Q What is your relationship to the defendant, Frank Derry?

A I am his brother.

Q How well do you know Frank?

A No one knows him better than I do, I think. We are only 18 months apart in age, and we spent our whole childhood together. I looked up to him, my big brother. We were best friends—didn't have many kids around us, so we stuck together. We went all the way through high school together until Fred dropped out in 11th grade to go to work at Nita Ford as a mechanic's apprentice. But since then we have remained close. We both live in Nita, and we get together at least every other week to do stuff with our families.

Q Do you have an opinion, based on your long association with Frank, about his character for violence?

A I sure do. Frank is a kind, gentle person. I have a really bad temper, but Frank always tried to show me how to stay calm and take a deep breath, count to 10, stuff like that. Even when other kids would do stuff to him that would make anyone mad, I never saw him lose his cool.

Q Have you ever seen him act violently towards Thelma or the kids?

A Never. He's a kind, gentle, loving husband and dad.

Q Can you give us some examples of how he behaves towards his wife and kids?

A He'll spend hours talking stuff over with Thelma—she complains a lot about how short of money they are, in a way that would drive me crazy pretty fast, I gotta admit—but Frank just keeps calm and keeps talking her down off her ledge. And he is amazingly patient with the three girls. He goes over their homework with them, and sometimes they back-talk to him but he just keeps helping them.

Q No more questions, Your Honor.

CROSS-EXAMINATION OF EDWARD DERRY:

Q When Frank was still in high school, you saw him have a fist-fight with another student, didn't you?

A Well, yeah, but it wasn't much of a fight.

Q The fight started because the other kid had insulted Frank's girlfriend, isn't that right?

A That's what I heard them arguing about when I saw them on the walkway, yeah.

Q Frank's voice was raised pretty loud, wasn't it—you could hear them from almost a block away, yes?

A True.

Q And in this fist-fight, the other kid used only his fists, didn't he?

A Yeah.

Q But Frank picked up a tree branch and slammed it into the kid's head, didn't he?

A Not real hard.

Q Hard enough that the kid landed in the hospital with a concussion, isn't that so?

A I did hear that, yeah.

Q No more questions.

THE WITNESS IS EXCUSED.

* * * * *

TRIAL TRANSCRIPT—DAY 6

In the Prosecution rebuttal case [assume that the Defense did not call Frank Derry as a Defense witness]:

DIRECT EXAMINATION OF GEORGE LYMAN:

Q How do you know the defendant Frank Derry?

A I work with him at Nita Ford.

Q What is your position there?

A I am the Service Department Manager, and Frank is one of my mechanics.

Q How long have you been his Manager?

A For the past seven years.

Q In that time, have you formed an opinion of Mr. Derry's character for truthfulness?

A Yes, I have. In my opinion Frank is not a very reliable person, not a man of his word. A lot of times he tells me reasons he had to miss a day of work for illness, but then I've caught sight of him in the park at lunchtime sitting on a bench having lunch with some lady or other.

Q With his wife Thelma?

A No, some other lady—and not always the same other lady, either.

Q How many times has that happened?

A Oh, at least 3–4 in the last two years.

Q Have you formed an opinion about his character for violence?

A Frank has a really bad temper, and when he flies off the handle he takes it out physically. I've had to warn him about not throwing tools around the shop or beating on the car he's working on. And I've seen him get pretty hot in arguments with co-workers.

Q Are you acquainted with Derry's next-door neighbor, Nat Rogers?

A Yes, he's a customer at Nita Ford, and I often write up his service orders for him and discuss his service needs.

Q As a result of your contacts with Mr. Rogers, have you formed an opinion of his character for violence—that is, whether he can be provocative or threatening when involved in an argument?

A Well, yes—you know how it is in the car business. Customers are often upset when their car has problems, and they don't like how much repairs cost these days. They are used to the old days when replacing an oil change cost $10, and they object when it costs $40 now—that's because we have to re-set the car's computer and run diagnostics for even a basic regular maintenance item like that.

Q Mr. Lyman, directing your attention back to the question of Mr. Rogers's character . . .

A I was getting to it. Sure, I've had a number of times when Mr. Rogers was upset with something we had done or some charge he thought was too much. But he never got angry—didn't raise his voice—and certainly never looked like he was going to get physical. Non-violent, I would call him. I wish I had more customers like him!

Q No more questions for this witness.

DEFENSE WAIVES CROSS-EXAMINATION; WITNESS IS EXCUSED.

[End of Exercise]

CHAPTER 5

IMPEACHMENT BY CHARACTER

I. TIPS & POINTERS

Rule 607. Who May Impeach a Witness

Any party, including the party that called the witness, may attack the witness's credibility.

Rule 608. A Witness's Character for Truthfulness or Untruthfulness

(a) Reputation or Opinion Evidence. A witness's credibility may be attacked or supported by testimony about the witness's reputation for having a character for truthfulness or untruthfulness, or by testimony in the form of an opinion about that character. But evidence of truthful character is admissible only after the witness's character for truthfulness has been attacked.

(b) Specific Instances of Conduct. Except for a criminal conviction under Rule 609, extrinsic evidence is not admissible to prove specific instances of a witness's conduct in order to attack or support the witness's character for truthfulness. But the court may, on cross-examination, allow them to be inquired into if they are probative of the character for truthfulness or untruthfulness of:

- **(1)** the witness; or
- **(2)** another witness whose character the witness being cross-examined has testified about.

By testifying on another matter, a witness does not waive any privilege against self-incrimination for testimony that relates only to the witness's character for truthfulness.

Rule 609. Impeachment by Evidence of a Criminal Conviction

(a) In General. The following rules apply to attacking a witness's character for truthfulness by evidence of a criminal conviction:

- **(1)** for a crime that, in the convicting jurisdiction, was punishable by death or by imprisonment for more than one year, the evidence:
  - **(A)** must be admitted, subject to Rule 403, in a civil case or in a criminal case in which the witness is not a defendant; and
  - **(B)** must be admitted in a criminal case in which the witness is a defendant, if the probative value of the evidence outweighs its prejudicial effect to that defendant; and

(2) for any crime regardless of the punishment, the evidence must be admitted if the court can readily determine that establishing the elements of the crime required proving—or the witness's admitting—a dishonest act or false statement.

(b) Limit on Using the Evidence After 10 Years. This subdivision (b) applies if more than 10 years have passed since the witness's conviction or release from confinement for it, whichever is later. Evidence of the conviction is admissible only if:

(1) its probative value, supported by specific facts and circumstances, substantially outweighs its prejudicial effect; and

(2) the proponent gives an adverse party reasonable written notice of the intent to use it so that the party has a fair opportunity to contest its use.

(c) Effect of a Pardon, Annulment, or Certificate of Rehabilitation. Evidence of a conviction is not admissible if:

(1) the conviction has been the subject of a pardon, annulment, certificate of rehabilitation, or other equivalent procedure based on a finding that the person has been rehabilitated, and the person has not been convicted of a later crime punishable by death or by imprisonment for more than one year; or

(2) the conviction has been the subject of a pardon, annulment, or other equivalent procedure based on a finding of innocence.

(d) Juvenile Adjudications. Evidence of a juvenile adjudication is admissible under this rule only if:

(1) it is offered in a criminal case;

(2) the adjudication was of a witness other than the defendant;

(3) an adult's conviction for that offense would be admissible to attack the adult's credibility; and

(4) admitting the evidence is necessary to fairly determine guilt or innocence.

(e) Pendency of an Appeal. A conviction that satisfies this rule is admissible even if an appeal is pending. Evidence of the pendency is also admissible.

You probably emerged from your studies of Rules 404–405 on character evidence with a sigh of relief, but recall that we deferred consideration of Rule 404(a)(3), which directs us to Rules 607–609, *i.e.*, the rules on impeachment of witnesses. Aside from the substantive use of the defendant's character (if opened up by him (404(a)(2)(A)), the victim's character (again, if opened up by the defendant (404(a)(2)(B)), the special rule for homicide cases (404(a)(2)(C)), and the special rules for sex offense and child molestation cases (412–415), this area of evidence law is the last remaining permitted use of "propensity" evidence—does the witness have a propensity to lie? Note that here the SOLE pertinent character trait of a witness, as a witness, is that witness's character for truthfulness.

Whenever a witness takes the stand in a civil or criminal trial he puts his credibility at issue. The common law developed many ways to suggest that a witness should not be believed, many of which are *not* character-related. These methods include showing that the witness has a poor memory, has limited vision, has a bias for or prejudice against one side or the other in the case, or has said inconsistent things about the facts on which he is now testifying. These methods enable the lawyer to say to the jury: "This witness is lying [or is mistaken] on this occasion, in this circumstance." As a general rule, the Federal Rules liberally permit these impeachment methods. Rule 613 imposes certain restrictions on the use of prior inconsistent statements.

But when it comes to *character-based* impeachment, the cross-examining lawyer is saying to the jury, "This witness is a liar by nature or character, and as such is *probably* lying right now." On the one hand, this type of evidence is more liberally admissible than character evidence on the historical merits. On the other hand, it is not as readily admitted as impeachment evidence that is not based on character reasoning. Again, this is because of the law's cautious approach to using evidence of a person's character, for fear that it will be misapplied or overvalued by the jury.[1] With Rules 608–609, as with Rules 404(a)(2)(A) and (a)(2)(B) and 405, careful adherence to the narrow limits of the rules will keep you out of trouble at trial.

Here are the points to keep in mind as you perform the exercises for this Chapter.

- Rule 608(a) allows you to present evidence of both a witness's reputation for truthfulness or untruthfulness, and of another witness's opinion of such witness's veracity.
- Beyond that, however, the Rule tries to ensure that the trial will not become a "mini-trial" on a witness's veracity. We do not want the jury to lose sight of its central task, that is, determining the facts on the historical merits. To minimize the risk that the jury will be distracted, although allowing cross-examination about a witness's specific untruthful acts that have not led to a conviction, Rule 608(b) forbids the opponent from presenting "extrinsic" proof of the act. If the witness admits the instance of truthfulness or untruthfulness, the cross-examining lawyer has achieved the best she can. If the witness denies it, the literal language of the Rule appears to leave the cross-examining lawyer with no recourse beyond closing argument: "[E]xtrinsic [*i.e.*, proof beyond the question put to the witness] evidence is not admissible to prove specific instances of a witness's conduct. . . ." Courts consistently bar calling other *witnesses* to contradict the witness's denial. However, some courts permit the cross-examiner to use a writing

[1] *See generally*, Advisory Committee Notes, Rule 404, 1972 Amendments.

reflecting the witness's untruthful act so long as the witness is competent to authenticate the writing, *e.g.*, the witness's own letter. *See* cases cited in Mueller & Kirkpatrick, *Evidence* § 6.27 at 498–9 (4th ed. 2009) (but noting the authors' view that "admitting . . . documents violates the Rule and invites reversal if the error is serious.").

- ➢ You may offer opinion or reputation evidence of a witness's *good* character for truthfulness to rehabilitate only after his veracity has been attacked on a *character-based* theory. Thus, evidence of a witness's poor eyesight would not open the door to reputation or opinion about the witness's *good* character for truthfulness.

- ➢ The only extrinsic evidence of a specific instance of conduct allowed to show bad character for truthfulness is evidence of a criminal conviction (such as a conviction record). Rule 609 defines the limits for attacking a witness's character for truthfulness by showing the witness's conviction of a crime. This is a fairly intricate rule, which you no doubt spent some time studying before turning to this book of exercises. For the exercises, keep these highlights in mind:

    - o The distinction between felony convictions under Rule 609(a)(1)) for any crime and convictions for *crimen falsi* under 609(a)(2). The latter type of conviction is automatically admissible. However, *crimen falsi* is a very narrow category of offenses; to fall within this category, the offense must include deceit as an essential element or, in the words of the statute, it must be "readily . . . determin[able] that establishing the elements of the crime required proof or admission of an act of dishonesty or false statement by the witness." The prevailing view is that without more, theft offenses do not qualify under 609(a)(2).

    - o The distinction in 609(a)(1) between felony convictions used against witnesses generally, which are subject to the standard Rule 403 balancing test (favoring admissibility), and those offered against a witness who is a criminal defendant, which are subject to a modified balancing test (favoring exclusion);

    - o In contrast, Rule 609(a)(2) convictions are not subject to a 403 balancing test; they are automatically admissible because the rule says they "must be admitted;"

    - o In administering the balancing test for a felony impeachment, most courts do not simplistically assume that "felony = probative of poor veracity, therefore admissible." Neither do they assume that if the felony conviction did not involve a crime suggestive of poor veracity, the conviction should be automatically excluded. Instead, many courts look to the so-called *Gordon*[2] factors: (1) the age of the conviction; (2) the extent to which the convicted person has led a "blameless" life since the conviction; and (3) whether the crime underlying the conviction carries a strong, weak, or no suggestion of lack of veracity. When the person being impeached is the criminal defendant, there are three further factors: (4) the similarity of the prior conviction's crime to the present charge, which increases the danger of the jury's misusing the prior conviction as propensity evidence on the merits—"he did it before, he probably did it here"; (5) the importance of the defendant's need to take the stand in his own defense (in some fact settings, the defendant may be the only witness who can give his side of "what happened"); and (6) pitted against the fifth factor, the importance to the prosecution of attacking the defendant's credibility (the case may become a "swearing contest" between the defendant and the prosecution's witnesses).

- Remoteness in time ordinarily reduces the probative value of evidence under the general 403 balancing test. However, Rule 609(b) prescribes a special balancing test when the item of evidence is a conviction. For a conviction more than 10 years old or as to which the release date from incarceration is more than 10 years old (whichever is later), there is a "reverse-403" balancing test: the probative value of the conviction must substantially outweigh the prejudicial effect of the conviction in order for the conviction to be admissible. Thus, the rule is heavily-tilted against admissibility;

➢ Criminal defense lawyers consider Rule 609 one of the most important battlegrounds in the landscape of criminal prosecution. (Again, the other "biggie" is Rule 404(b)'s "other purposes"—see discussion in Chapter 3 *supra*.) If the prosecution wins a ruling pre-trial that some or all of the defendant's convictions will be admitted, the case is likely to "plead out." If the defense wins a ruling excluding the convictions, going to trial is a more viable alternative for the defendant. Ordinarily, a criminal defendant can foreclose the prosecution from introducing his convictions under Rule 609 by the simple expedient of electing against testifying. However, suppose the defense succeeds in introducing a pretrial statement by the defendant as substantive evidence under the Excited Utterance hearsay exception. The introduction of the statement makes the defendant a hearsay

---

2 *Gordon v. United States,* 383 F.2d 936 (D.C. Cir. 1967), *cert. denied,* 390 U.S. 1029 (1968).

declarant, and under Rule 806 the prosecution is entitled to impeach his credibility. Hence, the prosecution could introduce the defendant's prior convictions under Rule 609 even though the defendant did not physically take the stand.

➢ When the witness is the criminal defendant or the crime victim, be aware that two sets of rules, Rules 404–05 *and* 608–609, are in play. For example, a defendant in a DUI case might succeed in excluding evidence of his conviction for reckless driving under Rule 609, given the similarity between the prior conviction and the charged crime. Nevertheless, depending on how the defense shapes its case, the prosecution still may argue that the defendant has put his character for careful driving in issue, opening the door to opinion or reputation evidence under Rules 404(a)(1) and 405. Even more creatively, the prosecution may contend that the prior conviction is admissible as a "non-character" Rule 404(b)(2) use—for example, in a second-degree murder prosecution arising from a traffic accident, to show the defendant's realization of the risks of speeding and, hence, the mens rea of recklessness. A knee-jerk reaction by defense counsel—"Your Honor has already excluded the prior conviction under Rule 609"—will betray counsel's ignorance of the subtleties of the interplay between the two sets of rules, thus making it harder to win the argument.

II. EXERCISE: IMPEACHMENT BY CHARACTER EVIDENCE

For the reasons discussed above, most battles concerning Rule 609 impeachments by conviction are fought pre-trial in motions *in limine.* Issues concerning Rule 608 testimony about a witness's truthfulness or untruthfulness may arise mid-trial, but often they too are dealt with in advance to ensure a smooth course of the trial. Accordingly, we will return here to the format of a pre-trial argument on motions for the simulations.

The professor will assign students to prepare brief memoranda of law in support of and in opposition to the following items of evidence, and then to argue the motions in class. Other students will be appointed as judges. As with the exercise in Chapter 1, no cases should be researched or cited (other than *Gordon* by reference to its factors); all arguments should be confined to the language of the applicable Rules and comments in the Advisory Committee Notes.[3]

1. In the criminal case, defense intends to call a witness, Claude DeKoonen, to testify that he was a member of the Novurbana Police Department for twelve years before turning to private

[3] We reiterate our acknowledgement in Chapter I's footnote 1: in "real life" no memorandum of law should be submitted without case research and citation. The limitation here is to keep life manageable and focused on close analysis of the Rules themselves.

security work. He will offer both his personal opinion, from working with Officer Lukasz, and Officer Lukasz's reputation within the department: that Lukasz was "careless with his investigations and his analysis of the facts." (You may omit consideration of the hearsay nature of the reputation evidence. You will see in your studies of the Rule 800 series that there is a limited hearsay exception for reputation).

2. In the civil case, defense intends to ask Lucia Beebe, if she is called as a witness for the plaintiffs: "Isn't it a fact that you have failed to pay business license fees, for which you were cited three times?"
3. In the civil case, plaintiffs intend to ask defendant Derry on cross-examination: "You were convicted in YR-9 of felony aggravated assault, weren't you?" (See Chapter 9 on Authentication; Ex. B is Derry's Arrest and Conviction Record.)
4. In the criminal case, if Derry takes the stand the prosecution intends to question him about both his YR-9 conviction for felony aggravated assault and his YR-4 conviction for tax fraud/perjury. (See Chapter 9—Authentication—Ex. B is Derry's Arrest and Conviction Record.) If he denies the convictions, the prosecution plans to offer his Arrest and Conviction Record in evidence. (Omit any consideration of authentication and hearsay; confine your arguments to admissibility under Rules 608 and 609.)
5. In the criminal case, the defense intends to offer Edward Derry's opinion of Thelma Derry's truthfulness. The defense states it believes it likely the court will allow neighbors to testify about what they heard passing between Frank Derry and Thelma in arguments. Accordingly, the defense proposes to have Edward Derry impeach Thelma's credibility by his opinion that "Thelma is a deceitful, lying, vengeful person who has the long knives out for Frank."
6. In the criminal case, the prosecution counters that if defense is permitted to elicit Edward Derry's opinion of Thelma's credibility, it will ask him on cross-examination: "You have heard, haven't you, that in YR-1, Thelma received the PTA Award for 'Distinguished Contribution to School Morale by a Parent'?" The prosecution will also offer the Award plaque itself in evidence.

[End of Exercise]

CHAPTER 6

OPINION

I. TIPS & POINTERS

Rule 701. Opinion Testimony by Lay Witnesses

If a witness is not testifying as an expert, testimony in the form of an opinion is limited to one that is:

- **(a)** rationally based on the witness's perception;
- **(b)** helpful to clearly understanding the witness's testimony or to determining a fact in issue; and
- **(c)** not based on scientific, technical, or other specialized knowledge within the scope of Rule 702.

Rule 702. Testimony by Expert Witnesses

A witness who is qualified as an expert by knowledge, skill, experience, training, or education may testify in the form of an opinion or otherwise if:

- **(a)** the expert's scientific, technical, or other specialized knowledge will help the trier of fact to understand the evidence or to determine a fact in issue;
- **(b)** the testimony is based on sufficient facts or data;
- **(c)** the testimony is the product of reliable principles and methods; and
- **(d)** the expert has reliably applied the principles and methods to the facts of the case.

Rule 703. Bases of an Expert's Opinion Testimony

An expert may base an opinion on facts or data in the case that the expert has been made aware of or personally observed. If experts in the particular field would reasonably rely on those kinds of facts or data in forming an opinion on the subject, they need not be admissible for the opinion to be admitted. But if the facts or data would otherwise be inadmissible, the proponent of the opinion may disclose them to the jury only if their probative value in helping the jury evaluate the opinion substantially outweighs their prejudicial effect.

Rule 704. Opinion on an Ultimate Issue

(a) In General—Not Automatically Objectionable. An opinion is not objectionable just because it embraces an ultimate issue.

> **(b) Exception.** In a criminal case, an expert witness must not state an opinion about whether the defendant did or did not have a mental state or condition that constitutes an element of the crime charged or of a defense. Those matters are for the trier of fact alone.

At trial, we generally allow witnesses to relay only facts they personally know; their personal opinions—inferences they have drawn from facts in the case—are inadmissible. The rationale is that it is the jurors' province to decide which inferences to draw from the factual testimony they choose to believe. Therefore, objections such as "calls for speculation," "lack of personal knowledge," or "improper opinion," should be made whenever witnesses attempt to give their personal opinions about the facts of a case, rather than simply reporting the facts they know.

However, there are important exceptions. In addition to exceptions under various rules where opinion is allowed—such as when providing character evidence under Rule 405 (character traits of a person) or under Rule 608 (character for truthfulness of a witness), or judging handwriting under Rule 901(b)(2), Rules 701–706 set forth the main exceptions that allow a witness to provide opinion testimony. As we shall see, the key component is whether the witness's opinion would be "helpful to the jury" in assessing the facts of the case by providing an inference that the jury likely would not or could not draw equally as well on its own.

Article VII of the FRE governs two types of opinion: lay opinion and expert opinion. Compared to other topics (character and hearsay, for example), this area of evidence law is relatively straightforward. It is true that considerable subtleties arise when the issue in expert evidence is whether the technique or theory the expert proposes relying on passes muster under the *Daubert* standard, but that is beyond the scope of these beginning simulation exercises. For our purposes, the points you should bear in mind for the practice exercises are:

A. Lay Opinion Evidence [FRE 701]

- ➢ The lay (*i.e.,* non-expert) witness must testify from personal knowledge. Rule 701's insistence that the lay opinion be "rationally based on the witness's perception" is more than a mere repetition of Rule 602's requirement for every witness's testimony (other than an expert or a party-opponent whose statement is offered under Rule 801(d)(1)(A) or (B)). Rule 602 relates to the basis for lay opinion while Rule 701 concerns the form of the testimony. Also, the Rule's reference to "rationally based" imposes the requirement that the lay witness's opinion be on a subject within the ken of the ordinary person. Admissible lay opinions tend to fall into three categories:
- ➢ *(1) Collective Fact or Shorthand Rendition.* The lay opinion must be "helpful to clearly understanding the witness's testimony or to determining a fact in issue." When the facts underlying the lay opinion or impression are difficult or impossible to articulate, the opinion is a helpful way to relate to the jury the sum and

substance of the witness's testimony. "The collective facts doctrine recognizes this reality. One common example is lay testimony that someone was intoxicated. Here the witness is not confined to descriptions of glazed eyes, problems in speech or motor coordination, changes in behavior or mood or affect, but may say directly (assuming adequate observation and common experience) that the person seemed drunk or under the influence." Mueller & Kirkpatrick, *Evidence* § 7.4 at 627–28 (4th ed. 2009). The following are common illustrations:

—Speed and other measurements ("the car had to be going over 90 miles per hour");

—Physical states, such as intoxication or injury; and

—Personal emotions of others ("defendant looked really angry and then he went crazy"). Note the use of "looked," Since the witness cannot read a third party's mind, under Rule 602 the witness cannot directly speculate as to the third party's state of mind. However, based on the third party's demeanor, the witness can opine that the third party "appeared" or "seemed" to be in a certain frame of mind.

➤ *(2) Skilled Lay Observer.* While most lay opinions are of the "collective facts" variety on topics such as age, speed, and weight, there are also "skilled lay observer" opinions. The foundation requires proof of repeated prior opportunities for observation. For instance, to authenticate a letter, the proponent might call the purported author's secretary who has seen the author write his signature on countless occasions. See Rule 901(b)(2). Or suppose that the witness is very familiar with a person. The witness would be permitted to opine about the person's sanity: "He was nuts; he wasn't all there."

➤ *(3) Valuation.* The courts often permit owners to testify to lay opinions about the value of their property or services: "I'd think my house is worth about $200,000." Lay opinion may not be "based on scientific, technical, or other specialized knowledge." If that is the basis of the opinion, Rule 702 governs, and the proponent will need to lay a different, much more extensive foundation.

➤ As a matter of advocacy, to the extent feasible it is helpful for the lay witness to articulate as many underlying facts as she can to support the opinion. Do not be content to lay a minimally sufficient foundation. The more sensory experiences a witness recounts in his testimony, the more likely the jury is to conclude that the witness is describing accurately an event she actually experienced. Compare these two versions of the same testimony about an actor's intoxication:

—"I don't know why, but he sure seemed drunk to me."

—"He was lurching from side to side, he sounded like he had a mouth full of mush, and he was yelling obscenities at the top of his lungs. First he wanted to fight me, and then just a little later he started crying and telling me how sorry he was. I thought he was drunk as a skunk."

B. Expert Opinions [FRE 702–703]

- An expert can be used at trial in four different ways:
  - to testify to a fact under Rule 602—the fact that the witness has a Ph.D. does not render her incompetent to testify to a fact that a percipient witness with a high school diploma could describe;
  - to give a lay opinion about a fact under Rule 701—in this respect, the witness is not opining in an expert capacity;
  - to give the jury a general lecture about a theory or technique;[1] or,
  - to derive an expert opinion about the significance of the facts in the case by applying a general theory or technique to the specific facts.

The last is by far the most common use of experts. When the expert testifies in this fashion, the expert's direct examination has an essentially syllogistic structure. A syllogism consists of the major premise, a minor premise, and a conclusion. For example, a psychiatrist might testify: If a patient displays symptoms A and B, the patient is suffering from mental disorder C (the major premise); this patient's case history includes symptoms A and B (the minor premise); and therefore, the patient suffers from disorder C (the conclusion). After the witness qualifies herself as an expert, the witness describes the general theory or technique she is relying on. Next the expert specifies the case-specific data that she will use the theory or technique to evaluate. Finally, the expert states the conclusion derived by applying the major premise to the minor premise.

As you have seen in your Evidence class and readings, today Rule 702(c) governs the types of theories and techniques that an expert may use as her major premise. Before the enactment of the Federal Rules, most jurisdictions followed the *Frye* test; to serve as a major premise at trial, a scientific theory or technique had to be generally accepted within the relevant expert fields. However, in 1993 in *Daubert v. Merrell Dow Pharmaceuticals, Inc.*, 509 U.S. 579 (1993), the Supreme Court held that the Federal Rules had impliedly abolished the *Frye* test. The Court construed the reference to "scientific . . . knowledge" in Rule 702 to mean that the expert's technique or theory must be reliable in the sense that it is supported by sufficient, methodologically sound empirical data and

---

[1] The Advisory Committee Note to Rule 702 explains that the drafters included the language "or otherwise" in the wording of the rule to make it clear that the expert does not have to offer an opinion applying the general theory or technique to the specific facts of the case. The expert can limit her testimony to an exposition of the theory or technique.

reasoning. The Court listed a number of factors such as testing and error rates that the judge should consider in deciding whether proffered scientific testimony is sufficiently reliable. Although *Daubert* dealt only with purportedly scientific testimony, Rule 702 refers in the alternative to "scientific, technical, or other specialized knowledge." In 1999 in *Kumho Tire Co., Ltd. v. Carmichael,* 526 U.S. 139 (1999), the Court ruled that whether the nature of the witness's testimony is "scientific, technical, or knowledge," the proponent must show that the underlying theory or technique is reliable; the requirement for a showing of reliability applies across the board. The Court added, though, that in the case of non-scientific expertise, the factors listed in *Daubert* might be inapplicable; it can be difficult to fit a square technical peg into a round scientific hole. The Court announced that in the case of non-scientific expertise, the trial judge has discretion to select the factors that are reasonable indicia of reliability.

Although many *in limine* motions targeting scientific testimony turn on Rule 702(c) it would be impractical to delve into those issues in this short text. Consequently, the exercises in this chapter concentrate on the other components of the expert's direct examination: the witness's qualification as an expert (702), the minor premise (703), and the wording of the final opinion (704).

- Leaving *Daubert* issues aside, the lawyer opposing an expert should be watchful on three fronts:
  - The expert will have been qualified only in a specified area or areas of expertise. Watch out for the witness who tries to exceed the bounds of her expertise to offer opinions on other matters. For example, assume a prosecution for assault on a police officer, where the defendant had been stopped on suspicion of drunk driving and allegedly punched the arresting officer. The defendant claims that he did not assault the officer, but was merely waving his arms to fend off the officer's overly aggressive arrest tactics. A toxicologist, after qualifying to state an opinion on the defendant's Blood Alcohol Level and presence of cocaine, might be asked, "What effect does such a BAL and cocaine levels have on a person's readiness to engage in belligerent behavior?" Opposing counsel should object, "Beyond the expert's field of qualification. The witness is a toxicologist, not a psychiatrist or psychologist."
  - Under FRE 703 an expert is allowed to rely on three types of sources for the case-specific information underlying her opinion: (1) personal observation, (2) facts stated to her in a hypothetical question incorporating other witnesses' past or expected testimony; and (3) certain types of out-of-court information, often called secondhand reports. Although the last category of information is formally used for a non-hearsay purpose, the witness's mention of this type of information obviously strains the hearsay rule.[2] Therefore, Rule 703 imposes special restrictions on

[2] The conventional wisdom has been that the secondhand report is being used for a legitimate nonhearsay purpose under Rule 801(c). More specifically, it is logically relevant to show

this last category. It ordinarily allows the expert to describe only in general terms the types of information she relied on and to inform the jury of the reasons why such information is considered a justifiable basis for an expert opinion, *provided* she establishes that it is the customary (reasonable) practice in her specialty to consider that type of information." The Rule prohibits the expert from detailing the contents of the information unless the proffering party satisfies the court that "their probative value in assisting the jury to evaluate the expert's opinion substantially outweighs their prejudicial effect." Thus, opposing counsel should be alert whenever the expert attempts to recount or quote any outside information. For example, in the DUI/assault-on-officer hypo above, the toxicologist might testify: "When I run a test after a roadside stop, it is important for me to have all the information about the subject's behavior during the stop. Different factors can affect the readings of the test results—for example, if the subject over-exerts during a heel-to-toe test, the Intoxilyzer readings have to be adjusted to compensate. So I always ask the officer to describe the event to me. That's what I was trained to do, and that's a routine practice among toxicologists. So far, so good. However, suppose at this point the toxicologist attempts to quote what the officer told her about the defendant's conduct. That attempt should prompt an objection. The objection might prompt an ensuing argument concerning the balance of probative value versus prejudicial effect—note that it is a "reverse-403" test, where the proponent of the evidence must persuade the court that the probative value of the facts or data substantially outweighs its prejudicial effect. Judges usually allow the proponent to go into chapter and verse about the content of the secondhand report only if the jury must know the detailed content of the report to understand the expert's reasoning and the contents of the report do not coincide with one of the central, disputed issues on the historical merits.

- Like lay opinions, the expert's opinion must "help the trier of fact to understand the evidence or to determine a fact in issue." FRE 702. Again, as noted earlier, Rule 704 allows an expert to express an opinion on "the ultimate issue." Often, however, the witness tries to overreach and opine on a matter of law or an issue well within the jury's ability to assess. As an example, an accident reconstruction expert may explain skid marks, vectors, road cambers, and the ultimate resting places of the vehicles—all to teach the jury how those elements of accident reconstruction help

---

its effect on the state of mind of the expert; the expert's receipt of the report makes his or her opinion better grounded. However, in dictum in Williams v. Illinois, 567 U.S. 50 (2012), five justices—Justice Thomas in concurrence and four dissenters, led by Justice Kagan—challenged the conventional wisdom; they forcefully argued that if the expert's opinion is conditioned on the secondhand report, the jurors cannot accept the expert's opinion without using the secondhand report for its truth. Some lower courts are now moving toward that view. People v. Sanchez, 63 Cal.4th 665, 374 P.3d 320, 204 Cal.Rptr.3d 102 (2016).

the expert determine where the vehicles were traveling, at what speeds, and how the crash took place. But if the expert adds, "Based on all of this, in my expert opinion the driver of the Fruehauf semi was negligent and caused the accident," what does that add to the scientific tutorial the expert has already given them? Nothing; it merely makes the expert a thirteenth juror. Therefore his opinion on the ultimate issue should be excluded as "not helpful." (A common version of this objection is "Invades the province of the jury.").

II. SAMPLE EXPERT WITNESS EXAMINATION

The following sample is taken from: Syd Beckman, Susan Crump, and Fred Galves, *Evidence: A Contemporary Approach*, 3d Ed., (West Academic Publishers) (2016), Chapter 12, "Witnesses: Opinion Testimony, Lay and Expert," ("Evidence Casebook") (with the page numbers from that casebook chapter referenced):

Evidence Casebook, pp. 529–536.

Direct Examination of Experts

HOW TO MAKE EXPERT WITNESSES CREDIBLE

By David Malone[3]

. . . You have experts testify because you hope that they will move the jury toward your client's position. They can do that only if their testimony is understandable and persuasive. With these two goals as our guide, let's examine the elements of presenting expert witnesses.

THE INTRODUCTION

Q. What is your full name, Dr. Jones?

Q. What is your business?

Q. How long have you been a research pathologist?

Q. What is your business address?

. . . Do not overlook opportunities to use the expert's titles ("doctor" and "research pathologist"); you are trying in every way possible to persuade jurors that this witness's knowledge is so different and better from theirs that they should pay special attention to what he has to say . . .

THE TICKLER

Q. Have you come to court today, Dr. Jones, prepared to state your expert opinion as a pathologist, on the cause of Harold Good's lung disease?

---

[3] David M. Malone is the senior litigation partner in the Washington D.C. office of Rivkin, Radler, Dunne & Bayh. He also lectures at the National Institute for Trial Advocacy and consults with law firms and government agencies on trial practice and strategy.

Prepare the expert to answer, "Yes, I have," to this question. You do not want him inadvertently to blurt out his opinion at this point—the jury is not yet ready for it, and you still have some dramatic interest to build before you reach the climactic moment when he gives his opinion.

. . . Many lawyers launch right into the expert's qualifications without reflecting on the fact that jurors have little understanding of why the expert is testifying and even less understanding of why they should listen to someone talk about where he went to school when they thought they were going to get evidence about a wrongful death.

Let them in on the secret. "This guy is here because he has the answer you jurors need." Perhaps this will heighten their interest in his qualifications, since they will now know why you re raising questions about them . . .

EDUCATIONAL AND WORK QUALIFICATIONS

Q. Before we get to your opinion, Dr. Jones, I would like to give us some information about your qualifications to give that opinion. Let's start with your education. Where did you go to college?

Q. What was your major at Cornell?

Q. What courses did you study that relate particularly to your examination of the cause of Mr. Good's death?

Q. Will you define "Organic Chemistry"?

Q. How does organic chemistry relate to the work you did in determining the cause of Mr. Good's death? (And so forth, highlighting courses that demonstrate his expertise in the area of testimony.)

Q. Let's turn now to your work experience as a pathologist. What was your first position in this field?

Q. How long did you do research for Mercy Hospital in Pittsburgh?

Q. Would you tell us about any responsibilities or experience you had at Mercy Hospital that would relate specifically to identifying the cause of Mr. Good's death? (And so forth, through the relevant work experience.)

Q. Dr. Jones, do you belong to any professional association?

Q. How did you become a member?

Q. Does the American Board of Pathologist have any activities that relate specifically to lung disease?

Q. What was your role in those activities?

Q. How do they relate to your work in this lawsuit?

To permit the expert to testify, the judge need only be persuaded that the witness has specialized knowledge that will help the jury in coming to a decision. As a technical matter, then, the qualifications could end when that minimal presentation has been made. That, however, would ignore the jury's need to develop confidence in the witness, to assess his credibility. If you demonstrate that the expert has had the relevant educational and work experience, jurors will be more willing to rely on the expert.

Again you need not cover all courses or all employment or all associations-just what is needed to meet the threshold requirements for admissibility and to make the expert a persuasive witness to the jury. Ask about associations where membership is by work review and invitation, not about those like the American Medical Association that accept payment of dues as the primary criterion for membership.

RESUME AND PUBLICATIONS

Q. Dr. Jones, let me hand you Plaintiff's Exhibit 47 for identification. Is that your current resume?

Do not call a resume a "curriculum vitae." Few if any jurors are comfortable with written Latin, even fewer with spoken Latin. Consider asking, "Is this a summary of your educational and work experience?" . . .

Q. Your Honor, I offer Plaintiff's Exhibit 47 in evidence.

Q. Dr. Jones, pages C through H of Plaintiff's Exhibit 47 are a listing of your publications, is that right?

Do not have the witness read and describe every item on the resume. You have already covered educational and work background . . .

Q. Some of those publications appeared in the *Journal of American Pathologist*. Please tell us what that journal is.

Q. What is a "peer review" journal?

Q. What significance does that have in evaluation the reliability of material published in such a journal.

Q. Who are the readers of that journal?

Q. Which of the publications you have written are particularly relevant to your work in determining the cause of Mr. Good's death?

Q. How does your August 1985 publication relate to the identification of the cause of lung disease? (And so forth, highlighting other relevant publication.)

[. . . Even if the other side stipulates (agrees) to your expert's qualifications], you should not dispense with presenting your expert's qualifications to the jury. Remember, [even if there is a stipulation] the court is merely saying that no in-court demonstration of qualifications is required to permit the witness to testify. Jurors still must decide how much weight to give the expert's testimony, [so they should hear something about educational and work background.]

. . . If your opponent rises during your qualification of an expert and offers to stipulate that the expert is qualified to testify, an effective response is:

Your Honor, we are happy to accept Mr. Barrister's statement that Dr. Jones is recognized as an expert in pathology and the determination of the cause of death in this type of case, and should be heard by the court and the jury. With the court's permission, we would like to present briefly some of his qualifications so that the jury can determine the weight to give his testimony.

With this, you have emphasized what appears to be opposing counsel's concession of the credentials of your expert, have highlighted your expert's expertise, and have turned aside your opponent's attempt to keep the jury from hearing about your expert's impressive qualifications. Of course, if you tell the court you will be brief, you must be brief . . .

THE TENDER

Counsel: Your Honor, I tender Dr. Jones to the court as an expert in the medical specialty of pathology and in the determination of the cause of disease and death in cases involving respiratory failure. Dr. Jones is qualified by reason of his education, experience, and research to provide expert testimony on the cause of the lung disease that resulted in Mr. Good's death.

Some jurisdictions require such a formal tender, others permit but do not require one, and the rest do not permit one. Judges who do not permit a formal tender have two concerns: They do not want to appear to be putting the court's imprimatur on an expert by ruling on the tender, and they do not like lawyers making speeches about evidence or witnesses before the jury. Some judges avoid the "imprimatur" problem by saying, "You may proceed, counsel."

Where permitted, a tender is often greatly appreciated by the court, because it spells out the scope of the expert's experience and testimony, making it easier to rule on admissibility. Also, the tender tolls the time for opposition to the expert; the court will be impatient with an opponent who sits quietly after a tender and later tries to argue that the witness is not qualified. (Of course, testimony that goes beyond the qualifications or tender is subject to challenge and additional voir dire). . . .

[Note that opposing counsel is allowed at this point to interrupt the witness' direct examination and "voir dire" the witness, where opposing counsel gets to cross-examine the witness on whether his qualifications are sufficient to be accepted as an expert witness before he provides his expert opinion. If opposing counsel had to wait until the witness completed his direct exam, the judge might later have to ask the jury to disregard an expert witness' entire testimony if the witness is not deemed qualified. This is an exception to the usual practice that opposing counsel must wait to cross-examine a witness until the witness completes direct examination.]

THE OPINION

Q. Dr. Jones, we have now reviewed your educational, work, research and experience in the medical area of the pathology of lung diseases. Based on that background, do you have an opinion that you hold with reasonable degree of medical certainty on what caused Mr. Good's death?

Q. What is that opinion?

Now you have arrived at the question you hope the jury has been waiting for: What killed Good? In preparing for trial, caution the expert to answer only "yes" to the first question, so that when he gives the opinion it stands out. The first question of this pair is designed to remind the jury of the reason for going through the credentials and to satisfy the technical requirements that an expert's opinion be based on an appropriate degree of certainty.

The required qualifying language—"reasonable degree of medical certainty"—varies from jurisdiction to jurisdiction (somewhere else, it might be "degree of certainty appropriate in the medical field of pathology"), but always the language must assure the court that the foundation for the expert's opinion is at least as firm as that which pathologist would require for conclusions reached in medical contexts. Thus, the requirement dovetails neatly with that in Rule 703 requiring that the bases of an expert opinion be of a type reasonably relied on by experts in the field. The first requirement goes to the strength with which the opinion is held; the second, to the bases supporting it. . . .

As you complete one major opinion, together with its bases and subordinate opinions, and move to the next, help jurors to organize the testimony in their minds (or their notebooks in enlightened jurisdictions) by using a transitional statement:

Q. Dr. Jones, have we now discussed all the bases for your opinion that Harold Good died of advanced lung disease?

Q. Let's turn then to the question of whether the lung disease was caused by exposure to coal dust from the Carbonblack Mine. Based on your background and on the work you did for this lawsuit, do you have an opinion on that which you hold with a reasonable degree of medical certainty?

This transitional statement also prompts the witness to leave one area and to follow your lead into the next, while allowing you to restate the expert's opinion in an unobjectionable way.

THE BASES

The questions allowing the witness to explain the bases follow a formula: "What did you do? Why did you do this? What did you find? What does that mean to you?" This formula is an attempt to anticipate the order and content of the questions jurors are asking themselves as they listen to the expert.

Q. Will you list for us the bases for your opinion that Harold Good died from lung disease?

Q. Turning to the first of the bases you have stated, the visual observation of the lung tissue during the autopsy: How did you examine the tissue?

Q. Why did you examine the tissue?

Q. What did you observe during the examination?

Q. How does the observation of blackened lung tissue support your conclusion that lung disease caused Mr. Good's death?

Q. Now, the second basis that you listed is the chemical analysis of the deposits found in the lung tissue. Why did you have a chemical analysis done?

Q. How was that analysis done?

Q. What were the results of that analysis?

Q. How does the identification of the black deposits as carbon particles support your conclusion that Mr. Good died of lung disease?

If the expert has several bases for a major conclusion, consider presenting them on a chart, a slide, or an overhead projection. You might even want to arrange the exhibit so that one basis at a time can be highlighted for the jury [using computer exhibits].

Do not spring the graphics on the court. At the pretrial, let the court know what chart, slide, or diagram you intend to use, [and make sure to lay a proper foundation for it under Rule 901.]

Under Federal Rule of Evidence 705, the bases need not be disclosed on direct examination. An opinion without articulated bases that are logical and reliable is, however, not very persuasive.

ANTICIPATING THE DEFENSE CASE

Q. Dr. Jones, have we now discussed all your bases for concluding that Harold Good died as a result of lung disease caused by exposure to coal dust that he inhaled during his years as a miner in the Carbonblack Mine?

Q. In coming to your opinion, have you considered the fact that Mr. Good had been a pack-a-day smoker for the last 50 years of his life?

Q. What effect does that fact have on your conclusion that he died because of exposure to coal dust in the mine?

Q. Why?

Q. Did you also consider that Harold Good had lived his entire life in the industrial area of Scranton, Pennsylvania?

Q. Does that fact cause you to change your conclusion that he died because of exposure to coal dust from the mine?

Q. Are you also familiar with the opinions on this question held by Dr. Smith, the pathologist who will be presented by the Carbonblack Mining Company? (Or were you present in court for the testimony of Dr. Smith?)

Q. Does Dr. Smith's opinion cause you to change your expert opinion that Harold Good died as a result of lung disease caused by coal dust from the Carbonblack Mine?

Q. Why not?

Q. Did you have to make any assumptions in coming to your conclusion?

Q. What assumption did you make?

Q. Why did you assume that?

Q. What effect does that assumption have on your analysis?

Q. What effect would an opposite assumption have had on your analysis?

You should know what the likely lines of cross-examination will be. Unless you have some reason to believe that the cross-examiner will avoid or miss certain lines of attack, you are better off raising them on direct. On direct examination your expert can deal with problematic questions in a no adversarial context. If the challenges go to the alleged unreliability of certain bases, deal with those when the particular basis is discussed.

By this approach, you show the jury that your witness is honest and open to considering all the pertinent information, favorable and unfavorable, and you defuse the impact of cross examination. You also boost your own credibility. Redirect examination does provide an opportunity to address problems that developed during cross-examination, but the strictures on redirect limit your opportunity to present the most persuasive and organized answer to the challenges. Anticipating the defense case may save you the time and expense of presenting additional expert testimony on rebuttal.

CONCLUSION

Some lawyers attempt, through their experts, to arm jurors with sufficient expertise to enable them to comprehend and evaluate the evidence relating to the relevant scientific issues. The risk with this approach is that these "newly trained experts" may, in the jury room, evaluate the underlying evidence for themselves without the benefit of the real expert's training and experience.

Other lawyers believe that the best approach is to persuade jurors to trust the expert rather than form their own conclusions. This is the better approach. Jurors need not understand organic chemistry in order to accept expert testimony on chemical tests as significant and consistent with recognized authority.

If expert testimony is well-organized, interesting, and supported by graphic displays that make it more memorable, you will have a better chance to persuade jurors.

[One last thing, try to resist the temptation that you, as the attorney, are also now an expert in the expert witness' field of expertise. Lawyers are expert advocates, but they should leave other areas of expertise to the experts. You do not need to become an expert in the field yourself to question an expert effectively. Instead, rely on your own expert to help you understand only those areas that are critical.] . . . In addition to defining the scope of the expert witness expertise, it is also critical to determine whether the area of witness' expertise is a legitimate field of knowledge that will be helpful to the jury.

In both lay opinion and expert testimony, the opinion given must be "helpful" to the jury. Recall that "helpful to the jury" means that the opinion has to give the jury more than a guess as to what happened—it must be an educated guess based on some key facts or expert analysis beyond the jury's knowledge. This is a decision the judge must make in her discretion, which usually is an easy decision when it comes to lay opinions. The more difficult determination is whether an expert's opinion is helpful to a jury. The problem lies in distinguishing between an expert's "specialized knowledge," which would be helpful to the jury, and what is merely "junk science," designed to manipulate the jury with something that only appears to be specialized or scientific, but really is not. It is where the witness is attempting to pass off a version of the events that is nothing more than just a guess, with no real helpful scientific, technical or specialized knowledge. Courts have been grappling with this issue since at least the beginning of the last century.

III. EXERCISE: OPINION EVIDENCE: (1) LAY OPINION; AND (2) EXPERT OPINION

The in-class exercise for this Chapter consists of playing a video excerpt from the civil case. Thus, all students in the class will be reacting without pre-preparation to the evidence offered. One-half of the class will be assigned to object on behalf of the party opposing the evidence—the available objections will be:

For lay opinion:

—"Lack of first-hand knowledge [not based on the witness's perception]."

—"Improper lay opinion—no showing of [adequate opportunity to observe / adequate experience]."

—"Improper lay opinion—the subject described does not fall within common lay experience."

—"Improper lay opinion—the subject of the opinion is scientific [technical, specialized]."

—"Improper lay opinion—the subject of the opinion is not helpful to the jury as the facts it is based on can be fully articulated to the jury such that the jury is competent to draw its own inferences."

For expert opinion:

—"Beyond the scope of this witness's area of expertise."

—"The proponent has not presented admissible evidence of every element of the hypothesis posed to the witness."

—"The proponent has not established that it is the customary practice in the expert's specialty to consider this type of out-of-court report."

—"The expert is seeking to disclose inadmissible underlying evidence forbidden by Rule 703."

—"The expert is offering an opinion on the ultimate issue that is not helpful to the jury [that invades the jury's province]."

The rest of the class will be asked to justify the admissibility of any of the challenged testimony.

CHAPTER 7

HEARSAY—DEFINITION

I. TIPS & POINTERS

Rule 801. Definitions That Apply to This Article; . . .

(a) Statement. "Statement" means a person's oral assertion, written assertion, or nonverbal conduct, if the person intended it as an assertion

(b) Declarant. "Declarant" means the person who made the statement.

(c) Hearsay. "Hearsay" means a statement that:

(1) the declarant does not make while testifying at the current trial or hearing; and

(2) a party offers in evidence to prove the truth of the matter asserted in the statement.

Any time a witness proposes to relate a written or oral statement made by a person outside court (more precisely, when that person is not on the witness stand while making the statement), the question arises whether the statement constitutes inadmissible hearsay. At trial we generally want to hear directly from a witness who has relevant (FRE 401) personal knowledge (FRE 602) and who can be cross-examined right then and there, enabling the jury (or a judge in a bench trial) to immediately assess that witness's credibility (FRE 607–613). In-court testimony about an out-of-court statement can constitute hearsay even when the witness is describing his or her own out-of-court statement. Therefore, if an out-of-court statement is related in court by a witness who merely heard or read the declarant's out-of-court statement, and that statement is offered to prove *as true* what the declarant asserted, the statement must be tested to determine if it *is* hearsay and, if so, if it is *admissible* (under an exemption or exception) or *inadmissible.*

This book includes three chapters on hearsay: this current chapter on The Definition of Hearsay; the following chapter on Hearsay Exemptions; and the next chapter on Hearsay Exceptions.

II. THE DEFINITION OF HEARSAY

The following exercises are designed to focus your attention on the aspect of Hearsay Definition—the aspect of hearsay law that beginning lawyers find most challenging. Assume that an out-of-court statement was an intended assertion and that it was made by a "declarant" (an out-of-court speaker or actor [*i.e.,* for non-verbal assertions]). Even then, many hearsay objections come to grief on the rocks of a third issue: is the out-of-court statement being offered in court to prove the "truth of the matter asserted in the statement"? "TMA" (TMA is evidence buffs' shorthand for "truth of the matter asserted") trips easily off the tongue once you learn how to recognize it; the trick is developing the experiential skill of recognition. Two alternative methods of formulating the same basic question may be helpful:

- "Who is the real witness?" Do we need to believe only the person on the stand recounting the out-of-court assertion or, in addition, the out-of-court person who made the assertion?
- To employ the fact that the out-of-court person asserted for the use the proponent is offering it, does the jury need to be able to assess the credibility/sincerity/accuracy of the out-of-court speaker/actor?

Under either of these formulations or the traditional "TMA," the recognition task boils down to this question: what uses are NOT for TMA? This leads to the standard list of "non-hearsay uses" of out-of-court statements. As we shall see, they tend to fall into three categories: mental output, verbal act, and mental input.

- "***MENTAL OUTPUT***" or "circumstantial evidence of state of mind" of the speaker or writer—the fact that the declarant uttered the words tells us something relevant about her thoughts, mood, or mental processes.
  - For example, assume Becky is about 5 feet tall. Janice (the witness) testifies in court that Ricardo (the declarant) told her outside court, "Becky is 7 feet tall." Declarant Ricardo's out-of-court statement to Janice that Becky is 7 feet tall may or may not be hearsay; it depends on how it is being used by the proponent, that is, the lawyer eliciting Janice's testimony about Ricardo's statement that Becky is 7 feet tall. If the lawyer is trying to prove that Becky is actually 7 feet tall, Ricardo's out-of-court statement is hearsay. The "real witness" about Becky's height is Ricardo. The jury must be able to assess Ricardo's credibility/sincerity/accuracy to determine if Becky is or is not 7 feet tall. But if the lawyer is eliciting Janice's description of Ricardo's statement to prove only that Ricardo is a very bad judge of height, or that he does not even really know Becky, the out-of-court statement is not hearsay. The only "real witness" here is Janice: if the jury believes her when she testifies to what she heard Ricardo say, the jury may then legitimately use Ricardo's statement to determine whether Ricardo is confused, mistaken, or a bad judge of height, etc. For this use, the jury needs to assess only Janice's credibility, not Ricardo's (except in the negative: his statement is being used to show that he is NOT credible on the subject of Becky's height.

  - If the declarant said, "I am Elvis Presley reincarnated," and a witness heard that statement, the witness could repeat the statement in court, not to prove that the person actually was Elvis reincarnated, but simply as circumstantial evidence that the declarant was delusional.

- Another variation of the "mental output theory" is the impeachment use of a witness's *prior inconsistent statements*—*i.e.*, pretrial statements inconsistent with his trial testimony. The inconsistency of the statements gives us an insight into the witness's state of mind. The argument is that if the witness tells two (or more) differing stories, the witness is either uncertain or lying. The "real witness" is the person who heard the witness earlier say the inconsistent statement. The out-of-court words are not being offered "for their truth." (But see a different use of a prior inconsistent statement that IS "for its truth"—FRE 801(d)(1)(A)—*infra*, Chapter 7.) The fact *of* the inconsistent statement is relevant to the witness's credibility even if the facts asserted *in* the statement are false.
- "***VERBAL ACTS***" or "legally operative acts"—the mere uttering (or writing) of the words, or the mere action (*e.g.*, handshake), constitutes a relevant element of the proofs in the case. For example, if a declarant makes an offer or an acceptance to a contract and a witness hears or reads the declarant's words of offer or acceptance, the witness can testify as to what the declarant said; it is being used only to prove the *fact* of the making of the offer or acceptance. Under the objective theory of mutual assent (remember Contracts?), legal consequences flow directly from the fact that the words constituting the offer or acceptance were uttered. The only "real witness" is the person who heard or read the legally-operative words spoken or written, *i.e.*, the witness on the stand. The same analysis applies when the witness testifies to a libelous out-of-court writing or a slanderous out-of-court oral statement.
- "***MENTAL INPUT***" or statements used for their "effect on state of mind of the listener"—assume that in a child custody case the mother wants to prove that the couple's young daughter is afraid of her father. The mother's attorney calls the girl to the stand to testify that her father told her that he killed her little brother. This is not hearsay so long as the purpose is not to prove that the father killed the brother, but only to prove the effect on the listener, *i.e.*, the girl. The fact that she heard her father make the statement explains why she was so fearful of violence from her father. The "real witness" is the little girl; the issue is whether she heard those words, and she is on the witness stand where her credibility can be assessed. The question is NOT whether the assertion by the declarant father was actually true. The father

might have lied to her about the little brother's death for the very purpose of frightening her.

- Statements offered to show notice are a variation of the "effect on the listener theory." A passerby told a shopkeeper, "Your sidewalk has slippery ice on it and someone walking along here could get hurt." Such would be hearsay if offered to prove there was dangerous ice on the sidewalk, but not if offered to prove that the shopkeeper was aware of a possible dangerous condition on his property and negligently failed to cure it. Anyone who heard the passerby's words could testify to what he heard the passerby say; he is the "real witness" as to whether the words of warning to the shopkeeper actually were spoken.

➢ Watch out for tricky cases—they can be fun. A little boy had been injured two years ago and alleges in his lawsuit that he cannot speak due to the trauma. A witness testifies that he heard the boy, just last week, say, "I can speak" (ignore for the moment the statement of a party opponent exemption, Rule 801(d)(2)(A))—or even, "I cannot speak." Neither utterance would be hearsay. The "real witness" is the person who heard the boy engaged in the act of speaking. The boy's very act of speaking disproves his claim that he cannot speak. The "truth" of his ability to speak does not depend on his sincerity/accuracy/credibility, but on the fact that words issued from his mouth—HE SPOKE (a "verbal act" in the literal sense)! Whose credibility needs to be assessed in order to use the evidence for this purpose? The answer is: the hearer's—and she is on the stand where her credibility/sincerity/accuracy can be assessed.

➢ In the final analysis, determining whether the statement is being used TMA requires careful, exhaustive analysis of the logical relevance of the statement. More specifically, you have to identify all the theories on which the statement is logically relevant in the case. In many cases, the statement is logically relevant on more than one theory. On some theories, the statement might be hearsay while on other theories it will be nonhearsay. If so, on one theory it could be admissible nonhearsay while on another it is inadmissible. If so, the judge ordinarily resolves the problem by admitting the statement for the nonhearsay purpose with a Rule 105 limiting instruction.

III. EXERCISE: THE DEFINITION OF HEARSAY—TRUTH OF THE MATTER ASSERTED

For each short hypo below based on the Case Files, develop: (a) your initial reaction as to whether it is for TMA and (b) your reasoned-out argument why it is or is not for TMA. You may find that your initial reaction is reliable—that's good. You may find that your initial reaction misleads you—it's good to find that out and guard against it. The more practice you have, the easier it will be to recognize legitimate nonhearsay theories. Like identifying form objections, recognizing hearsay is an experiential skill. In some cases, you may find that there are good arguments for both sides: it both IS and IS NOT for TMA. If so, develop both arguments. (Then you can always get a job with one side or the other.)

For all these hypos, do not concern yourself with whether the evidence offered may be a candidate for a hearsay "exemption" (see Chapter 7—for example, as a statement of a party opponent) or "exception" (see Chapter 8). Confine your analysis to the threshold question of whether the statement/action is being offered for TMA. Also, do not concern yourself with whether the evidence is arguably inadmissible on another ground, *e.g.*, FRE 403, 411, 404, etc. In this chapter, we want to focus narrowly on the threshold question because, as previously stated, this is the hardest aspect of hearsay law for neophyte litigators to master.

1. In the civil case, plaintiff Rogers testifies that he heard defendant Derry shouting at Thelma the morning of the day the fire happened, "I hate your guts, Thel—I wish you were dead!"

2. In the civil case, Rogers testifies that later that same day Thelma told him that Derry had piled up six cans of gasoline in the sun porch of their house.

3. In the civil case, Rogers testifies that the day after the fire, when he and his wife Frederica were viewing the wreckage, Frederica said, "That SOB Derry is going to pay for this—for what he did. It's bad enough he mistreats Thelma the way he does—but now he's gone and almost killed his family and he's ruined everything we built up here as our home. I just want to lay down and die. . . ." and then she burst into tears and collapsed in a heap among the ashes of their home.

4. In the civil case, Derry testifies that two days after the fire, Rogers's wife Frederica told him, "Nate is a basket case over this fire damage, but I'm like a Phoenix, rising from the ashes—nothing can keep me down." Then she started to sing "Tomorrow" from the Broadway musical *Annie* ("The sun'll come out tomorrow—bet your bottom dollar that tomorrow there'll be sun!").

5. In the criminal case, Rogers testifies that one week before the fire he said to Derry, "You should check out the special they are having on home fire alarm systems at Home Depot." And that Derry replied, "Why don't you mind your own business and keep your nose out of mine!"

6. In the criminal case, Thelma testifies as a witness for the prosecution. She recites that two days before the fire she told Derry she had been to see a lawyer to talk about starting divorce proceedings.

Now that you are getting the hang of making and responding to objections to hearsay that raise the TMA issue, we will turn to an actual portion of the trial proceedings. But this time, you will not be reading the transcript to analyze it. Instead, students will be appointed as examining lawyer and witness, and a student as judge, to bring the trial alive for you. The professor will appoint members of the class to react to the proceedings as opposing counsel, to object to any arguably hearsay testimony. Those members will have to identify the hearsay, either in the question (in which case say "Objection, Your Honor, the questions calls for hearsay.") or in the answer (in which case say "Objection, Your Honor, the witness's testimony constitutes hearsay, move to strike.") and oppose its admission. The examining lawyer will prepare to defend the admissibility of the testimony sought. *In all cases, the ONLY issue to be argued is whether the testimony DOES or DOES NOT involve an attempt to prove TMA.* You may assume and use any facts from the *civil-case* exercises from preceding weeks. However, do not use any facts from the preceding weeks' *criminal-case* exercises.

CHAPTER 8

HEARSAY EXEMPTIONS

I. TIPS & POINTERS

Rule 801. . . . Exclusions from Hearsay

. . . .

(d) Statements That Are Not Hearsay. A statement that meets the following conditions is not hearsay:

(1) ***A Declarant-Witness's Prior Statement.*** The declarant testifies and is subject to cross-examination about a prior statement, and the statement:

(A) is inconsistent with the declarant's testimony and was given under penalty of perjury at a trial, hearing, or other proceeding or in a deposition;

(B) is consistent with the declarant's testimony and is offered to rebut an express or implied charge that the declarant recently fabricated it or acted from a recent improper influence or motive in so testifying; or

(C) identifies a person as someone the declarant perceived earlier.

(2) ***An Opposing Party's Statement.*** The statement is offered against an opposing party and:

(A) was made by the party in an individual or representative capacity;

(B) is one the party manifested that it adopted or believed to be true;

(C) was made by a person whom the party authorized to make a statement on the subject;

(D) was made by the party's agent or employee on a matter within the scope of that relationship and while it existed; or

(E) was made by the party's coconspirator during and in furtherance of the conspiracy.

The statement must be considered but does not by itself establish the declarant's authority under (C); the existence or scope of the relationship under (D); or the existence of the conspiracy or participation in it under (E).

Certain types of out-of-court statements used for the truth of the matter asserted are not considered hearsay, even though the statements technically fall within the definition of hearsay. These doctrines are, definitionally, hearsay "exemptions."[1] Although hearsay exemptions function similarly to hearsay exceptions, they are not so categorized under either Rule 803 (23 exceptions), 804(b) (5 exceptions), or 807 (see the next chapter on "Hearsay Exceptions"). On the Multistate Bar Examination, when the correct answer relies on one of these exemptions, the correct answer often states only that the statement is "admissible nonhearsay." As you know, the two categories of these exemptions are "Prior Statements" [FRE 801(d)(1)] and "Statements of a Party Opponent" [FRE 801(d)(2)].

A. Prior Statements [FRE 801(d)(1)]

A "declarant" who has made an out-of-court statement can later become the witness who is asked to repeat on the stand his own pretrial statement. Even though that witness can be cross-examined now about his extra-judicial statement, that prior statement still is considered hearsay because it was an out-of-court statement when the declarant-witness originally made it. The common law preferred immediate cross-examination. The declarant who was not on the stand when he made the statement could not be so examined at that time; one might say he can be examined only "retrospectively." The common law wanted to assure the examiner the opportunity to "strike while the iron was hot." The common law did not want to permit the witness to frustrate the cross-examiner by retreating behind the claim that they could no longer recall the event they described in their statement.

However, there are three instances when such prior statements by a declarant-witness are admissible as nonhearsay under the rule: 801(d)(1)(A)—Prior Inconsistent Statements (provided they were made "under penalty of perjury at a trial, hearing, or other proceeding or in a deposition"); 801(d)(1)(B)—Prior Consistent Statements (provided they are offered in response to an "express or implied charge that the declarant recently fabricated [his consistent testimony on direct examination] or acted from a recent improper influence or motive in so testifying); and 801(d)(1)(C)—Statements of Prior Identification.

For our practice exercises, keep in mind the following points about these three types of "Prior Statements of a Witness":

- First, for all three types of prior statements, the declarant must testify as a witness in court and be subject to cross-examination about her prior statement(s). In other words, a prior statement made by a declarant who is *not* now testifying as a witness and subject to cross-examination cannot qualify for admission under FRE 801(d)(1).

---

[1] The FRE and many lawyers and commentators call them "exclusions," but that term risks the misunderstanding that they are *not allowed* under the hearsay rules, as opposed to the true fact that they *are allowed*, precisely because they have been freed from the hearsay restriction. They are also sometimes referred to as "non-hearsay," or "not hearsay by definition."

- FRE 801(d)(1)(A) Prior Inconsistent Statement. Distinguish between the nonhearsay use of a prior inconsistent statement solely to impeach a witness (attacking the witness's credibility because he has said inconsistent things) and a prior inconsistent statement admitted to prove the truth of what the declarant asserted.

- The following example helps clarify the difference between Rule 613 impeachment and a substantive use under Rule 801(d)(1)(A). Hector stated in his pre-trial deposition that he had four beers on the night of the accident. However, at trial Hector says he did not drink any alcohol at all that night. Hector has made a prior inconsistent statement because his trial testimony does not match his deposition testimony. In this example, the prior statement can serve two purposes. First, Hector can be impeached under FRE 613. In this analysis, Hector's prior inconsistent statement is not hearsay because it is being used only to impeach his current testimony—he has said different things about the same topic, suggesting he is either uncertain or untruthful; but it is not being offered to prove that he actually drank four beers. But second, Hector's prior statement can ALSO be used to prove that he *did* drink four beers (the TMA in the prior statement). The statement satisfies the three conditions imposed by 801(d)(1)(A); Hector made his prior inconsistent statement: (1) under penalty of perjury, (2) at a deposition (the analysis would be the same if his prior testimony had been at a "trial, hearing, or other proceeding"), and (3) Hector can now be cross-examined at trial.

- A prior inconsistent statement need not be 100% diametrically opposed to the current testimony in order to be considered "inconsistent." The statements do not need to be flatly "contradictory." If a witness said previously that the defendant was in the bar the night of the incident but now says that either the defendant or his brother—"sitting here today I can't be sure"—was at the bar, the previous statement would be sufficiently inconsistent with his current testimony, even though it is also partially consistent. The same inconsistency standard governs whether the statement is used only for impeachment or as substantive evidence.

- ALL three conditions prescribed by Rule 801(d)(1)(A) must be met. For example, although an affidavit may be given under penalty of perjury, it does not meet the requirement that it was given at a trial, hearing, deposition, or other proceeding; therefore, it is not admissible under the Rule. The police cannot render a witness's pretrial statement admissible as substantive evidence by the simple expedient of administering an oath to a witness during a stationhouse interrogation. A police interrogation does not qualify as a formal "proceeding."

- FRE 801(d)(1)(B) Prior Consistent Statement. Now contrast a Rule 801(d)(1)(A) prior INCONSISTENT statement with a Rule 801(d)(1)(B) prior statement that is CONSISTENT with the witness's trial testimony. Assume that Lisa, an alibi witness, testifies at trial that the defendant, Bob, was with her in New York on the night the victim was assaulted in Sacramento. On cross-examination, the prosecution asks her, "Isn't it a fact that four weeks ago, Bob gave you a $5,000 bribe to lie for him and testify that he was with you in New York on the date of the assault?" On redirect, Lisa testifies that she took no bribe from Bob, and further that she had told police officers two months ago (*i.e.*, before the alleged bribe) that Bob had been with her in New York. Although Lisa's recitation of her out-of-court statement to the police would otherwise be hearsay, it qualifies as an admissible prior consistent statement. The statement is highly probative because it antedates the alleged bribe; the timing suggests that the witness did not give the testimony *because of* the bribe.

- The timing here is critical. If we change the hypo and Lisa offers to testify to a statement about Bob and New York that she made only two weeks before trial (*i.e.*, after the alleged bribe), the prior consistent statement will NOT be admissible. Just as it raises doubt about subsequent trial testimony, the bribe calls into question any post-bribe statement. Although the text of Rule 801(d)(1)(B) is unclear on this point, the Supreme Court read in the temporal priority doctrine in *Tome v. United States*, 513 U.S. 150 (1995).

- In 2014, this provision was amended. As amended, the provision also applies when the statement is offered "to rehabilitate the declarant's credibility as a witness when attacked on another ground." The accompanying Advisory Committee Note states that "[t]he intent of the amendment is to extend substantive effect to consistent statements that rebut other attacks on a witness—such as the charges of inconsistency or faulty memory."

- FRE 801(d)(1)(C) Prior Statement of Identification. The third type of prior statement that would otherwise be hearsay but is treated as a hearsay exemption is a witness's prior identification of a person. Think of this rule as a special kind of prior consistent statement that does not require a charge of recent fabrication or improper influence or motive as under Rule 801(d)(1)(B). Assume that Ben is charged with assault. At trial an eyewitness to the assault, Casey, takes the stand to testify. If Casey made an out-of-court identification of Ben at a line-up, the identification is a "statement," either because he said, "That's the guy I saw assaulting the victim," or he pointed to Ben at the line-up in response to the police's question whether he recognized anyone in the line-up as the attacker. The statement ordinarily would fit the definition of hearsay if offered to prove that Ben was the assailant, but under Rule 801(d)(1)(C) it is admissible as a prior identification.

- Do not confuse the differences among subsections (A), (B), and (C) of the Rule. Casey's prior identification of Ben as the assailant need not have been made under penalty of perjury at a legal proceeding (unlike Rule 801(d)(1)(A)). Furthermore, it need not be used to rebut a charge of recent fabrication or improper influence or motive (unlike Rule 801(d)(1)(B)).

In all three exemptions under 801(d)(1), someone other than the declarant/trial witness can testify to the declarant's prior inconsistent statement, prior consistent statement, or prior identification, provided the declarant-trial witness testifies at the trial and is subject to cross-examination concerning the prior statement. Suppose, for example, that on the stand at trial Casey is uncertain—or even unable—to identify Ben as the assailant as he looks at him at the defense table. In that event, an officer who was present at the pre-trial line-up can take the stand to testify that Casey identified Ben in the line-up, provided Casey can be re-called to be cross-examined if the defense so chooses. For an extreme example, *see United States v. Owens*, 484 U.S. 554 (1988)(a pretrial identification of an attacker was admissible even though the witness could no longer remember the attack itself).

B. Statements of an Opposing Party [FRE 801(d)(2)]

The rules also define a statement of an opposing party as nonhearsay, rather than as an exception to the hearsay rule. Although the original version of the Rule used the traditional common-law terminology describing these statements as "admissions of a party-opponent," the 2011 restyling changed the terminology to "statements of a party-opponent." The idea is that if a party makes a statement as a declarant, that party should be responsible for whatever he has said in the past and should not be permitted to hide behind the hearsay rule to render his previous statements inadmissible. The party is free to take the stand to deny or explain the statement. The five types of "statement of a party opponent" are set out in the five sub-parts of Rule 801(d)(2).

For our practice exercises, keep in mind the following points:

- For all five types, the word "admission," which used to appear in the Rule, often led students to think, erroneously, that the statement had to "admit" something. The 2011 restyling of the Rule deleted that word. The statement needs only to have been *made by* an opposing party and be relevant to some fact that the opponent has a right to prove at trial

- Category #1: Illustrating a statement made directly by the party herself [FRE 801(d)(2)(A)]: Assume that Pauline is sued for negligence in an accident in which she was the driver. Pauline was overheard telling her mother right after the accident that she was intoxicated while driving and that is why she lost control of her car. Pauline's out-of-court statement that she was intoxicated and that is what caused the accident can be used against Pauline in court by the plaintiff—Pauline's opponent—to prove that Pauline was negligent and caused the accident.

- Notice that the statement by Pauline is being used AGAINST Pauline by Pauline's opponent in the lawsuit. If Pauline had told her best friend that she was sober when she was driving, Pauline could not introduce that statement to help her case because the statement is not that of an "OPPOSING party." *This limitation is true for all five sub-categories of the rule.* Pauline would probably have to offer her own statement as a prior consistent statement, but we have seen that it is difficult to clear all the hurdles of Rule 801(d)(1)(B) to introduce a consistent statement as nonhearsay.

- <u>Category #2: Illustrating a statement the party has adopted as true or manifested her belief it is true [FRE 801(d)(2)(B)]</u>: Assume the same lawsuit. Right after the accident, a bystander says to Pauline, "You have been drinking, haven't you?" Pauline appears embarrassed and says, "Yes." Even though the person who said to Pauline, "You have been drinking, . . ." is not a party to the lawsuit, that person's statement is admissible against Pauline because Pauline "adopted" the statement of the person as her own by saying "yes." (The bystander's statement itself is offered for a nonhearsay purpose, that is, the effect on Pauline's state of mind ("mental input").) It would not be enough for Pauline to refer to or even quote the bystander's statement. The circumstances must support the inference that Pauline agreed with the substantive content of the bystander's statement.

- Pauline also might be deemed to have adopted the statement as her own even if she had simply remained silent and said nothing in response to the statement, if a reasonable person would have protested and immediately denied that the statement was true. The courts often say that they are admitting the evidence as a "tacit admission."

- <u>Category #3: Illustrating a statement by a person who was/is authorized to speak for the party [FRE 801(d)(2)(C)]</u>: Assume that in the same lawsuit Pauline's lawyer says at a press conference after a pre-trial hearing, "Pauline is very sorry about the accident, and she is now in rehab to work on her drinking problems so that she does not cause any more such accidents in the future." Even though Pauline's lawyer is not a party to the lawsuit, the lawyer's statement still can be used against Pauline as though Pauline herself had made the statement. Pauline authorized her lawyer to be her spokesperson with respect to the lawsuit. (This doctrine poses an agency issue.) Be sure to determine whether the authorization to be a spokesperson on behalf of a party is broad enough to make any statement at all on behalf of the party, or whether the authorization is limited to a certain scope of topics.

- Category #4: Illustrating a statement by the party's agent or employee, made during the employment relationship and in the scope of that employment [FRE 801(d)(2)(D)]: Assume the same underlying facts as above, but plaintiff sues only Pauline's employer, South High School (not Pauline herself). Pauline was driving the School's van on a School field trip. After the accident, Pauline gets out of the van and says, "Boy, I should not have had all that vodka at the office just before driving here; that was dumb!" Plaintiff wants to use Pauline's statement against defendant High School. The High School objects on grounds of hearsay. As a quick review, distinguish this situation from the first three categories of 801(d)(2): (1) Because the High School did not directly make the statement itself, 801(d)(2)(A) does not apply; (2) because the High School did not adopt Pauline's statement as true or do anything to suggest that it believed the statement to be true, 801(d)(2)(B) is inapplicable; and, (3) because the High School did not authorize Pauline to serve as an official spokesperson for the High School, 801(d)(2)(C) does not apply. But Pauline is the defendant's employee-agent. Under 801(d)(2)(D), as long as Pauline's statement: (1) relates to duties within the scope of her employment (driving the school van on a field trip) and (2) was made during her employment relationship with the High School (Pauline was working for the School at the time), Pauline's statement can be admitted against the High School. However, if Pauline is the school custodian with no bus-driving responsibilities and she took the bus out on her own, her statement would not qualify under the rule, because the statement would not relate to her employment duties.

- Category #5: Illustrating a statement by a co-conspirator made during and in furtherance of the conspiracy [FRE 801(d)(2)(E)]: Assume that Pauline is criminally charged with methamphetamine drug distribution. Pauline's friend, Ringo, was caught in Mexico with drugs, cash, and guns on him. Earlier, during an arranged buy of drugs, he told an undercover police officer, "I am going to drop some meth off at Pauline's house so that Pauline can be the northern California distribution center for your gang as long as you guys bribe the Feds to keep them off our backs." Even if co-conspirator Ringo is not charged with any crime, Ringo's statement to undercover police can still be used against defendant Pauline, as long as there is evidence (a) of a drug conspiracy that (b) Pauline and Ringo were members of, and (c) that Ringo's statement to undercover police was made during, and (d) to further, the conspiracy. (The statement was to undercover police, whom Ringo thought were fellow criminals. If he had made the statements to police whom he knew to be police, the statements would not have been "in furtherance of the conspiracy.")

- Finally, with respect to the last three types of statements of a party opponent, where someone is standing in the shoes of the party opponent—(C) an authorized spokesperson, (D) an agent/employee, or (E) a co-conspirator—the foundational facts set out in each sub-section cannot be supplied solely by the hearsay statements being offered. Those facts must be corroborated by independent evidence other than the hearsay statements.

Most courts hold that a statement of a party-opponent under Rule 801(d)(2) is not subject to Rule 602's requirement of first-hand knowledge, at least for personal statements admitted under (d)(2)(A) and adoptive admissions admitted under (d)(2)(B); *see, e.g., United States v. Hernandez,* 105 F. 3d 1330 (9th Cir. 1996), *cert. denied,* 522 U.S. 890 (1997); *Mahlandt v. Wild Canid Survival & Research Center, Inc.*, 588 F.2d 626 (8th Cir. 1978). Similarly, a party-opponent's personal and adoptive admissions are generally treated as free from Article VII's restrictions on opinion evidence. These rules reflect the generally permissive nature of the party-opponent exemptions from hearsay: if the party-opponent said it, he is free to take the stand to explain why it should not be taken as true.

II. EXERCISE: HEARSAY EXEMPTIONS: (1) PRIOR WITNESS STATEMENTS; AND (2) STATEMENTS OF A PARTY-OPPONENT

The in-class exercise for this Chapter consists of the playing of a video excerpt from the criminal case. Thus, all students in the class will be reacting without pre-preparation to the evidence offered. One-half of the class will be assigned to objection on behalf of the party opposing the evidence—the objection will be "Hearsay!"—but the challenge to the objector will be to meet the arguments made by the offering party. The other half of the class will defend the admission of the evidence on either or both of two grounds: (1) the evidence is offered for a nonhearsay use, or (2) the evidence is admissible as a hearsay "exemption" under 801(d)(1) or (2).

CHAPTER 9

HEARSAY EXCEPTIONS

I. TIPS & POINTERS

Rule 802. The Rule Against Hearsay

Hearsay is not admissible unless any of the following provides otherwise:

- a federal statute;
- these rules; or
- other rules prescribed by the Supreme Court.

Rule 803. Exceptions to the Rule Against Hearsay—Regardless of Whether the Declarant Is Available as a Witness

The following are not excluded by the rule against hearsay, regardless of whether the declarant is available as a witness:

(1) ***Present Sense Impression.*** A statement describing or explaining an event or condition, made while or immediately after the declarant perceived it.

(2) ***Excited Utterance.*** A statement relating to a startling event or condition, made while the declarant was under the stress of excitement that it caused.

(3) ***Then-Existing Mental, Emotional, or Physical Condition.*** A statement of the declarant's then-existing state of mind (such as motive, intent, or plan) or emotional, sensory, or physical condition (such as mental feeling, pain, or bodily health), but not including a statement of memory or belief to prove the fact remembered or believed unless it relates to the validity or terms of the declarant's will.

(4) ***Statement Made for Medical Diagnosis or Treatment.*** A statement that:

(A) is made for—and is reasonably pertinent to—medical diagnosis or treatment; and

(B) describes medical history; past or present symptoms or sensations; their inception; or their general cause.

(5) ***Recorded Recollection.*** A record that:

(A) is on a matter the witness once knew about but now cannot recall well enough to testify fully and accurately;

(B) was made or adopted by the witness when the matter was fresh in the witness's memory; and

(C) accurately reflects the witness's knowledge.

If admitted, the record may be read into evidence but may be received as an exhibit only if offered by an adverse party.

(6) ***Records of a Regularly Conducted Activity.*** A record of an act, event, condition, opinion, or diagnosis if:

(A) the record was made at or near the time by—or from information transmitted by—someone with knowledge;

(B) the record was kept in the course of a regularly conducted activity of a business, organization, occupation, or calling, whether or not for profit;

(C) making the record was a regular practice of that activity;

(D) all these conditions are shown by the testimony of the custodian or another qualified witness, or by a certification that complies with Rule 902(11) or (12) or with a statute permitting certification; and

(E) neither the source of information nor the method or circumstances of preparation indicate a lack of trustworthiness.

(7) ***Absence of a Record of a Regularly Conducted Activity.*** Evidence that a matter is not included in a record described in paragraph (6) if:

(A) the evidence is admitted to prove that the matter did not occur or exist;

(B) a record was regularly kept for a matter of that kind; and

(C) neither the possible source of the information nor other circumstances indicate a lack of trustworthiness.

(8) ***Public Records.*** A record or statement of a public office if:

(A) it sets out:

(i) the office's activities;

(ii) a matter observed while under a legal duty to report, but not including, in a criminal case, a matter observed by law-enforcement personnel; or

(iii) in a civil case or against the government in a criminal case, factual findings from a legally authorized investigation; and

(B) neither the source of information nor other circumstances indicate a lack of trustworthiness.

Rule 804. Exceptions to the Rule Against Hearsay—When the Declarant Is Unavailable as a Witness

(a) Criteria for Being Unavailable. A declarant is considered to be unavailable as a witness if the declarant:

(1) is exempted from testifying about the subject matter of the declarant's statement because the court rules that a privilege applies;

(2) refuses to testify about the subject matter despite a court order to do so;

(3) testifies to not remembering the subject matter;

(4) cannot be present or testify at the trial or hearing because of death or a then-existing infirmity, physical illness, or mental illness; or

(5) is absent from the trial or hearing and the statement's proponent has not been able, by process or other reasonable means, to procure:

(A) the declarant's attendance, in the case of a hearsay exception under Rule 804(b)(1) or (6); or

(B) the declarant's attendance or testimony, in the case of a hearsay exception under Rule 804(b)(2), (3), or (4).

But this subdivision (a) does not apply if the statement's proponent procured or wrongfully caused the declarant's unavailability as a witness in order to prevent the declarant from attending or testifying.

(b) The Exceptions. The following are not excluded by the rule against hearsay if the declarant is unavailable as a witness:

(1) ***Former Testimony.*** Testimony that:

(A) was given as a witness at a trial, hearing, or lawful deposition, whether given during the current proceeding or a different one; and

(B) is now offered against a party who had—or, in a civil case, whose predecessor in interest had—an opportunity and similar motive to develop it by direct, cross-, or redirect examination.

. . .

(3) ***Statement Against Interest.*** A statement that:

(A) a reasonable person in the declarant's position would have made only if the person believed it to be true because, when made, it was so contrary to the declarant's proprietary or pecuniary interest or had so great a tendency to invalidate the declarant's claim against someone else or to expose the declarant to civil or criminal liability; and

(B) is supported by corroborating circumstances that clearly indicate its trustworthiness, if it is offered in a criminal case as one that tends to expose the declarant to criminal liability.

We have now covered what hearsay IS; what uses of out-of-court statements are NOT for the truth and therefore not hearsay; and what uses are for TMA but are NOT HEARSAY by virtue of their status as "hearsay exemptions." We now turn to the last question: even if it IS hearsay, is it nevertheless admissible as an exception?

Of the total of twenty-nine exceptions enumerated in the Rules—23 in Rule 803, five in Rule 804, and a residual one in Rule 807—we will concentrate on the most commonly invoked ten: Rule 803(1)–(8) and Rule 804(b)(1) and (3). Of course, you will want to be familiar with the others.[1] However, you need greater familiarity with the exceptions you are most likely to encounter in the courtroom.

The exercises simulating how these exceptions arise at trial follow after Chapter 9—Authentication, in an overall "wrap-up" video segment covering the main evidence topics we have addressed in the exercises. Your professor may even use the final video as a tool for course review before examinations. Looking ahead to that exercise, here are the points to keep in mind about hearsay exceptions:

- Do not immediately rush to the exceptions. Be sure you have first analyzed whether the challenged evidence even fits the definition of hearsay. For example: Does the out-of-court statement contain any intended assertion—801(a)? Is it being offered only for a nonhearsay purpose ("not for TMA")—801(c)? Does it fall within a hearsay exemption—801(d)? Only after you have passed through all these way-stations should you begin searching for an exception. Invoking a hearsay exception should be your last resort (when you are preparing in advance of trial, you should always analyze the evidence for arguably applicable exceptions—see below on "objection-proofing" your examination outlines).
- Conversely, even if you decide that the statement has a plausible and relevant non-hearsay purpose, do not stop there. Are you satisfied to have it admitted only "not for the truth"? Would you prefer to have it admitted for both purposes? If so, search for as many exceptions you can argue for without losing credibility.
- Avoid the mistake of the beginning lawyer who boldly cites "the unavailability exception—the declarant is sick/died/moved away,

[1] Without intending to play favorites, we mention Rule 803(21)'s importance when offering reputation evidence under Rule 405 or Rule 608. Rule 803(18) grants special permission to experts to cite to and quote from "learned treatises." Rule 803(22) allows prosecutors to avoid convoluted proofs based on prior convictions.

etc." There is no such animal. Rather, "unavailability" as defined under Rule 804(a) is a prerequisite to using any of the five exceptions enumerated in Rule 804(b).

- Likewise, do not misread Rule 803 as requiring "availability." It is true that the title of the Rules uses that term; however, the Rule merely provides that Rule 803 exceptions may be used regardless of the declarant's availability or unavailability.
  - We leave *Crawford*[2] and its progeny—regarding the interplay between hearsay law and the U.S. Constitution's 6th-Amendment Confrontation Clause—to your classroom studies.
  - You will have a better instinct for the interpretive issues that arise under an exception if you bear in mind the reasons why that exception was recognized in the first place. What "indicia of reliability" made the common-law courts sufficiently trusting of that type of out-of-court statement to allow it in for the truth? For example, a literal reading of Rule 803(4)'s exception for statements made for medical diagnosis or treatment would confine it to statements made by the patient herself. Yet, the exception has been interpreted to extend to statements made by the patient's family members, friends, and even "Good Samaritans." The circumstantial guarantee of the reliability of such statements is the desire to get sound medical treatment for the patient—and like the patient, some *persons* (e.g. the patient's family, friends, or even Good Samaritan strangers assisting the patient) *reporting on her behalf* will be motivated to provide accurate information. They want to help the doctor help their loved one. Thus, the more familiar you are with the underlying policy reasons supporting a rule, the better you will be able to argue for or against that rule's applicability in any given situation.

II. EXERCISE: HEARSAY EXCEPTIONS

When you are in trial, evidentiary issues can arise suddenly and in the heat of the battle. These are not ideal moments to try painstakingly to parse a hearsay exception into its component parts. When your opponent is urging the judge to exclude your hearsay evidence and you latch onto "excited utterance, Your Honor" like a dying man clinging to a life raft, it will be hard to keep all the requirements of Rule 803(2) in mind. However, there are three ounces of prevention that will serve you better than a pound of cure:[3]

First, "objection-proof" your examination outlines. Foresee every objection you think your opponent may make and note out your response

[2] *Crawford v. Washington*, 541 U.S. 36 (2004).

[3] The complexity of hearsay sparks this advice, but it applies equally to all areas of evidence law.

in advance. As the opponent, try to predict what the other side will try to get into evidence and prepare your objections *in advance*. What are your best counter-arguments to their best arguments for admissibility?

Second, trials are not a closed-book exam. Keep your pocket-size, well-annotated volume of FRE right out there on counsel table. Don't leave home—or go to trial—without it. In addition, have within easy reach your favorite evidence text that gives you a short but persuasive analysis of each rule.[4] Judges appreciate crisp arguments that cite the rule number and the rule's language—much more than they "appreciate" attorneys' personal opinions about, or paraphrases of, the rules. And when the evidentiary issue is crucial, come to court prepared with a case offprint, or even better a short memorandum of law ("points and authorities"), to hand to the judge in support of your argument. If you are ready to insert that into the record—for the benefit of the appellate court that can second guess the trial judge's ruling—the trial judge will know you mean business.

Third, you are busy enough juggling witnesses, exhibits, opposing counsel's interference, and the judge's wish to have you "keep it moving, counsel." Don't strain your memory. Use cheat sheets. For every hearsay exception that you expect you are likely to use, have a thumbnail précis of the rule clipped to your trial notebook. For example:

PSI - 803(1)
describing, explaining
event, condition
while or immed after (no time to concoct)
perceived it

Accordingly, your exercise for this chapter is to prepare and bring to class a "cheat sheet" for each of the ten exceptions that may be invoked in the final video: Rule 803(1)–(8) and Rule 804(b)(1) and (3), plus Rule 804(a) because it is a prerequisite to Rule 804(b)'s exceptions.

[End of Exercise]

[4] *E.g.*, Goode & Wellborn, *Courtroom Evidence* (2012–13 Stud. ed.); Imwinkelried, *Evidentiary Foundations* (10th ed. 2018); Mueller & Kirkpatrick, *Evidence* (4th ed. 2009).

CHAPTER 10

AUTHENTICATION

I. TIPS & POINTERS

Rule 901. Authenticating or Identifying Evidence

(a) In General. To satisfy the requirement of authenticating or identifying an item of evidence, the proponent must produce evidence sufficient to support a finding that the item is what the proponent claims it is.

(b) Examples. The following are examples only—not a complete list—of evidence that satisfies the requirement:

(1) ***Testimony of a Witness with Knowledge.*** Testimony that an item is what it is claimed to be.

(2) ***Nonexpert Opinion About Handwriting.*** A nonexpert's opinion that handwriting is genuine, based on a familiarity with it that was not acquired for the current litigation.

(3) ***Comparison by an Expert Witness or the Trier of Fact.*** A comparison with an authenticated specimen by an expert witness or the trier of fact.

(4) ***Distinctive Characteristics and the Like.*** The appearance, contents, substance, internal patterns, or other distinctive characteristics of the item, taken together with all the circumstances.

(5) ***Opinion About a Voice.*** An opinion identifying a person's voice—whether heard firsthand or through mechanical or electronic transmission or recording—based on hearing the voice at any time under circumstances that connect it with the alleged speaker.

(6) ***Evidence About a Telephone Conversation.*** For a telephone conversation, evidence that a call was made to the number assigned at the time to:

(A) a particular person, if circumstances, including self-identification, show that the person answering was the one called; or

(B) a particular business, if the call was made to a business and the call related to business reasonably transacted over the telephone.

(7) ***Evidence About Public Records.*** Evidence that:

(A) a document was recorded or filed in a public office as authorized by law; or

(B) a purported public record or statement is from the office where items of this kind are kept.

(8) ***Evidence About Ancient Documents or Data Compilations.*** For a document or data compilation, evidence that it:

(A) is in a condition that creates no suspicion about its authenticity;

(B) was in a place where, if authentic, it would likely be; and

(C) is at least 20 years old when offered.

(9) ***Evidence About a Process or System.*** Evidence describing a process or system and showing that it produces an accurate result.

(10) ***Methods Provided by a Statute or Rule.*** Any method of authentication or identification allowed by a federal statute or a rule prescribed by the Supreme Court.

Rule 902. Evidence That Is Self-Authenticating

The following items of evidence are self-authenticating; they require no extrinsic evidence of authenticity in order to be admitted:

(1) ***Domestic Public Documents That Are Sealed and Signed.*** A document that bears:

(A) a seal purporting to be that of the United States; any state, district, commonwealth, territory, or insular possession of the United States; the former Panama Canal Zone; the Trust Territory of the Pacific Islands; a political subdivision of any of these entities; or a department, agency, or officer of any entity named above; and

(B) a signature purporting to be an execution or attestation.

(2) ***Domestic Public Documents That Are Not Sealed but Are Signed and Certified.*** A document that bears no seal if:

(B) it bears the signature of an officer or employee of an entity named in Rule 902(1)(A); and

(C) another public officer who has a seal and official duties within that same entity certifies under seal—or its equivalent—that the signer has the official capacity and that the signature is genuine.

(3) ***Foreign Public Documents.*** A document that purports to be signed or attested by a person who is authorized by a foreign country's law to do so. The document must be accompanied by a final certification that certifies the genuineness of the

signature and official position of the signer or attester—or of any foreign official whose certificate of genuineness relates to the signature or attestation or is in a chain of certificates of genuineness relating to the signature or attestation. The certification may be made by a secretary of a United States embassy or legation; by a consul general, vice consul, or consular agent of the United States; or by a diplomatic or consular official of the foreign country assigned or accredited to the United States. If all parties have been given a reasonable opportunity to investigate the document's authenticity and accuracy, the court may, for good cause, either:

(A) order that it be treated as presumptively authentic without final certification; or

(B) allow it to be evidenced by an attested summary with or without final certification.

(4) ***Certified Copies of Public Records.*** A copy of an official record—or a copy of a document that was recorded or filed in a public office as authorized by law—if the copy is certified as correct by:

(A) the custodian or another person authorized to make the certification; or

(B) a certificate that complies with Rule 902(1), (2), or (3), a federal statute, or a rule prescribed by the Supreme Court.

(5) ***Official Publications.*** A book, pamphlet, or other publication purporting to be issued by a public authority.

(6) ***Newspapers and Periodicals.*** Printed material purporting to be a newspaper or periodical.

(7) ***Trade Inscriptions and the Like.*** An inscription, sign, tag, or label purporting to have been affixed in the course of business and indicating origin, ownership, or control.

(8) ***Acknowledged Documents.*** A document accompanied by a certificate of acknowledgment that is lawfully executed by a notary public or another officer who is authorized to take acknowledgments.

(9) ***Commercial Paper and Related Documents.*** Commercial paper, a signature on it, and related documents, to the extent allowed by general commercial law.

(10) ***Presumptions Under a Federal Statute.*** A signature, document, or anything else that a federal statute declares to be presumptively or prima facie genuine or authentic.

(11) ***Certified Domestic Records of a Regularly Conducted Activity.*** The original or a copy of a domestic record that meets the requirements of Rule 803(6)(A)–(C), as shown by a certification of the custodian or another qualified person that complies with a federal statute or a rule prescribed by the Supreme Court. Before the trial or hearing, the proponent must give an adverse party reasonable written notice of the intent to offer the record—and must make the record and certification available for inspection—so that the party has a fair opportunity to challenge them.

(12) ***Certified Foreign Records of a Regularly Conducted Activity.*** In a civil case, the original or a copy of a foreign record that meets the requirements of Rule 902(11), modified as follows: the certification, rather than complying with a federal statute or Supreme Court rule, must be signed in a manner that, if falsely made, would subject the maker to a criminal penalty in the country where the certification is signed. The proponent must also meet the notice requirements of Rule 902(11).

(13) ***Certified Records Generated by an Electronic Process or System.*** A record generated by an electronic process or system that produces an accurate result, as shown by a certification of a qualified person that complies with the certification requirements of Rule 902(11) or 902(12). The proponent must also meet the notice requirements of Rule 902(11).

(14) ***Certified Data Copied from an Electronic Device, Storage Medium, or File.*** Data copie4d from an electronic device, storage medium, or file, if authenticated by a process of digital identification, as shown by a certification of a qualified person that complies with the certification requirements of Rule 902(11) or 902(12). The proponent must also meet the notice requirements of Rule 902(11).

Article 9 of the FRE governs the topic of authentication of exhibits. This may be the most straightforward of all our topics: follow the recipes in the rules and you should have no trouble. The recipes are based on three basic principles.

First, focus on the basic purpose of authentication. That purpose will help you comply with the rules or argue for an extension or a narrower interpretation of a rule as a means of getting your evidence admitted (as the proponent) or excluded (as the opponent).

As stated in FRE 901, authentication requires the presentation of "sufficient [evidence] to support a finding that the item [being offered in evidence] is what the proponent claims it to be." In court, this is usually translated as "laying a sufficient foundation for the item of evidence." The judge does not decide whether the item is what it is claimed to be. Rather, the judge accepts the proponent's foundational testimony at face value and inquires only whether the testimony has sufficient probative value to allow the jury to rationally find that the item is what it is claimed to be. Thus, the judge plays a limited, screening role.

"Foundation" is most easily understood as "what you have to show in order to do what you want to do next." A contractor has to pour the foundation before she erects the first floor. What does this rule require me to show? As an example, under FRE 602 for every lay witness the witness's proponent must lay a foundation sufficient for the jury to find that the witness will testify from first-hand knowledge. Thus, in an intersection accident case, unless the first-hand knowledge is so evident that neither the court nor the opponent will raise an issue, the proponent should ask the witness:

Q Do you know the color of the light that was facing the Chevrolet?

A Yes. [Knowledge is shown.]

Q *How do you know?*

A I was standing on the corner and saw the light as the Chevrolet drove into the intersection. [First-hand nature of knowledge is shown.]

Q What color was the light for the Chevrolet?

A Green.

When it comes to exhibits, the "recipe" for the foundation may be found in:

- Rule 901(b)'s list of specific types of adequate authentication for various types of items (documents via handwriting; voice; telephone conversations; public records; ancient documents; data compilations; processes or systems);
- Rule 902's list of types of evidence that are "self-authenticating" (where the foundation is located within the document itself and/or other circumstantial evidence regarding the document), including properly certified copies of official records under Rule 902(4) and properly certified business records under Rule 803(6) that fit under Rule 902(11); and,
- For types of evidence not specifically covered by Rules 901–02, to comply with Rule 901's general requirement of "sufficient evidence," the resourceful attorney has two options: (1) devise her own solution by asking herself, "What will satisfy this judge that I am showing enough to let him admit this evidence?", or (2) turn to her library for texts and treatises that illustrate proper foundations.[1] The attorney is not limited to the specific examples listed in Rule 901(b). They are merely illustrative. The attorney has adequately authenticated an exhibit whenever she marshals

[1] *See, e.g.*, Imwinkelried, *Evidentiary Foundations* (10th ed. 2018); Imwinkelried & Leach, *California Evidentiary Foundations* (5th ed. 2018). For a discussion of the foundation for computer animations and the overall admissibility of computer animations in general, *see* Galves, *Where-the-Not-So-Wild-Things-Are: Computers in The Courtroom, The Federal Rules of Evidence, and the Need for Institutional Reform and More Judicial Acceptance,* HARVARD JOURNAL OF LAW & TECHNOLOGY (2000).

enough circumstantial evidence to support a rational inference that the item is what she claims it to be.

Second, even if an item of evidence has been admitted in evidence because the court has ruled the foundation sufficient, the jury needn't accept the item as true, trustworthy, or even authentic. The jury, as the trier of fact, has the ultimate job under Rule 104(b) of deciding whether to credit and trust the evidence. Thus, even after losing the fight to exclude the item on the ground of inauthenticity, the opponent of the item of evidence may still win the war by adducing testimony convincingly challenging the item's authenticity and reliability.

Third, never forget that even after you have surmounted the most obvious admissibility barrier (*e.g.,* authentication); all of the other rules still apply. Evidence analysis is like conditions analysis in Contract law. To activate a contract duty, you have to fulfill or excuse every condition to the duty. Similarly, if three foundations apply to an item—*e.g.,* authentication, Original Documents, and hearsay—the proponent has to be prepared to lay all three foundations. Similarly, as the opponent, you must consider all avenues of attack. For example, imagine that you, the defense in the criminal case, want to offer a letter from Derry to his wife in which he professes his undying love for her. You want to use the letter to counter the prosecution's theory of motive based on marital discord and Derry's alleged concern about the financial impact of a divorce action. If you call Derry as a witness, authenticating the letter as his will be easy:

Q Mr. Derry, who wrote this letter?

A I did.

Q Whose signature is this at the bottom?

A Mine.

Q Is this letter in the same condition as when you wrote it?

A Yes, nothing has changed.

Q When did you write that letter?

A (Some date well before the wife's death)

At this point, the requirement of authentication has been satisfied.[2] But now you will likely be met with your opponent's objection to the letter as hearsay: what Derry (the declarant) wrote in it was asserted out of court. It is not a statement of an opposing party, since the defense is offering it on behalf of Derry. How will you get it in? Moreover, assuming you overcome the hearsay obstacle, what if the letter is dated eight years before the fire? Is it relevant under Rule 401? Is it vulnerable under 403?

Two final points about authentication may help the beginning lawyer understand the variety of issues that can arise.

---

[2] Even if you decide to exercise Derry's Fifth Amendment right not to testify and therefore do not call him, you will surely easily find someone who is familiar enough with his handwriting to authenticate his signature.

— Some exhibits "testify"—they offer substantive evidence. For example, under the "silent witness doctrine," a surveillance camera's film of the mugger at an ATM machine provides "testimony" about what the culprit looked like and what he did. Here the proponent claims that the film accurately depicts the mugger. For such kinds of exhibits, an extensive foundation will be required as to assure the reliability of the "testimony." Typically, the foundation involves proof of the process or system by which the film (or other medium) was made and details about how the equipment was maintained.[3] The lawyer must take a similar approach to authenticating an X-ray. Since no one can see what the X-ray depicts, the lawyer must validate the scientific process that produced the X-ray. The lawyer offering such evidence must research and prepare fully the detailed foundation required.

Other exhibits merely "illustrate" a witness's oral testimony. For example, an expert, while describing tests he performed on the tensile strength of steel construction materials, might draw a schematic diagram of the machinery used to do the tests, the placement of the materials in the testing machinery, and the places he looked on the steel for signs of stress or failure. His drawing itself does not "testify"—only he does; but his drawing helps the jury follow and understand his testimony. Here the proponent claims only that the diagram accurately depicts the witness's description of the machinery, etc.[4] For such "illustrative" exhibits, a much less formal foundation is normally required.

Between these two poles there is a great variety of exhibits—called by some courts and commentators "demonstrative," "illustrative," etc.—as to which there is a similar variety of foundational requirements. Specific research into the specific type of evidence will assure the best chance of admissibility.

— Some tangible evidence is the "real" thing (and therefore often referred to as "real evidence"): the gun used in a robbery-by-threat prosecution, for example. A new lawyer might assume that if the actual gun is not available at trial (allegedly disposed of by the defendant, perhaps), then no visual or tangible proof of the item is possible. That gap in evidence would hurt the prosecution case, because the crime involves as an element the use of a threatening

---

[3] For example, the foundation for a surveillance camera photograph would likely include: (1) How and when the film was installed; (2) how the camera was activated to take the photograph; (3) whether the camera was in good working order at the time and whether it actually took the photograph at the time and place in question; (4) whether the camera system was operated and maintained at the time by a qualified person; (5) how long after the incident the film was removed; (6) whether there a "chain of custody" of the film sufficient to show there was no opportunity to doctor or "photoshop" the photograph (although in many courts this goes only to weight, not to admissibility); and, (7) whether the film was properly developed after the incident.

[4] If the judge allows the diagram, the opponent of the evidence should consider requesting a limiting instruction to tell the jury how it may and may not use the diagram. Although they permit the use of the diagram in open court, some judges will not send the diagram to the jury for their use during deliberations.

weapon—thus the more threatening the weapon appears, the more likely the jury will find guilt. However, if the victim describes the appearance of the gun used during the crime and testifies that the exhibit is fairly similar to that gun, the judge may admit the "representative" gun as demonstrative evidence. The proponent is not claiming that the pistol *is* the pistol used in the crime, but only that the exhibit is generally similar to that pistol.[5]

II. SAMPLE FOUNDATIONS

The following discussion and question-answer samples are taken from: Syd Beckman, Susan Crump, and Fred Galves, *Evidence: A Contemporary Approach*, 3d Ed., (West Academic Publishers) (2016), Chapter 3, "Sources of Evidence: Physical Evidence," ("Evidence Casebook") (with the page numbers from that casebook chapter referenced at the beginning of each sample examination):

AUTHENTICATION—R. 901

Evidence Casebook, pp. 93–95

There are eight generally recognized steps to authenticating physical evidence at trial. The steps may vary slightly from courtroom to courtroom, but the basic procedure is the same.

1. Steps to Authenticating Physical Evidence.

Step 1: Have the evidence marked with an exhibit number or letter by the court reporter, if not done pre-trial;

FYI

All physical evidence is given an exhibit number or letter in sequence. Plaintiff's first exhibit is usually designated Plaintiff's Exhibit "1" or "A," and her second exhibit is designated Exhibit "2" or "B," and so on. However, the evidence need not be offered sequentially. The same marking procedure applies to the Defendant's exhibits. Once an exhibit has been marked, it is *always* referred to in court by its exhibit number or letter. This is because the appellate court does not have a video of the trial. When a lawyer hands a document to a witness, the appellate court has no way of knowing what the lawyer is showing the witness unless the lawyer calls it by its exhibit number or letter.

Step 2: Hand the exhibit to the opposing attorney for inspection [or send it electronically to counsel's computer screen];

Step 3: Then hand the exhibit to the authenticating witness [or send it electronically to the witness's computer screen];

[5] If the judge allows the representative gun, the opponent of the evidence should consider requesting a limiting instruction to tell the jury how it may and may not use the exhibit.

Step 4: Lay the foundation for its admission through witness testimony;

Step 5: Offer the exhibit into evidence;

Step 6: Wait for opposing counsel's objections, if any;

Step 7: If not forthcoming, ask the judge for a ruling on the exhibit's admissibility; and

Step 8: With the court's permission, hand the exhibit to the judge in a bench trial or to the jury by passing it among them [or send it electronically to the judge's/jury's computer screen] or have the witness read aloud from it if the exhibit is a document.

Practice Pointer

Inexperienced trial lawyers may sometimes forget to follow Step (5), offering the exhibit into evidence, or Step (7), asking for a ruling on admissibility, if the judge fails to rule. These omissions can lead to disaster. Evidence that is not offered and admitted by the judge is not considered part of the case and will not support a verdict, an omission that is sometimes learned about for the first time on appeal when one party challenges the sufficiency of the evidence.

Practice Pointer

When possible, make certain that you have enough copies of any particular piece of evidence so that the judge, jury, and opposing counsel may all have copies [or make sure the exhibit is accessible electronically to their computer screens—it is always a good idea to have hard copy back-ups in the unlikely event of a computer glitch].

2. Applying the Steps in Order to Authenticate a Murder Weapon.

Here is an example of how these steps might be followed when the prosecution wants to authenticate the actual murder weapon in a homicide case:

Prosecution: (Addressing the court reporter) Please mark this gun as State's Exhibit 1 **(Step 1)**. I now call Officer Tommy Thompson to the stand.

Prosecution: Please state your name.

Witness: Tommy Thompson

Prosecution: How are you employed?

Witness: I am a homicide detective here in the city of Madison.

Prosecution: Did you have an opportunity to be called to the scene at 113 Main Street on the evening of May 13, 2014 to investigate a homicide?

Witness:	Yes.
Prosecution:	Whose residence is that?
Witness:	The defendant, Mike Sutton's.
Prosecution:	As you were conducting your investigation at 113 Main, did you find any weapons relevant to this case?
Witness:	Yes, we found a .44 caliber Smith and Wesson gun in the defendant's pants pocket when we searched him.
Prosecution:	Your honor, may the record reflect that I am showing State's Exhibit 1 to opposing counsel for inspection. **(Step 2)**.
Prosecution:	Officer Thompson, I now want to give you what has been marked as State's Exhibit 1, a gun **(Step 3),** and ask—can you can identify it? **(Step 4)**.
Witness:	Yes. We found this .44 caliber gun on Mr. Sutton immediately after the shooting. **(Step 4)**.
Prosecution:	How do you know Exhibit 1 is the same gun you found on Mr. Sutton that evening? **(Step 4)**.
Witness:	Because I remember the serial number on the weapon, and this gun has those serial numbers.
Prosecution:	Your honor, I would like to offer State's Exhibit 1 into evidence **(Step 5)**.
Judge:	Any objections?
Defense Counsel:	No, your honor. **(Step 6)**.
Prosecution:	Is State's Exhibit 1 admitted into evidence, your honor? **(Step 7)**.
Judge:	Yes.
Prosecution:	You honor, may I publish the weapon to the jury? **(Step 8).** [Note, this would typically be done by showing the gun to the jury]

Evidence Casebook, pp. 109–111

A. Maps, Graphs, Charts, and Diagrams

Authentication of items such as maps, graphs, charts or diagrams is relatively simple. The elements of the foundation are testimony: (1) as to what the object represents; (2) that the witness is familiar with the object or what the object represents; (3) as to why the witness has that familiarity; and (4) that in the witness's opinion, the object is a fair and accurate depiction of that object or what that object represents. Despite the language of the predicate, this type of demonstrative exhibit does not need to be accurate nor created to scale to be admissible.

At some point, a lawyer may also want to have the authenticating witness leave the witness stand (with the court's permission) and mark on the map, graph, chart, or diagram to illustrate his testimony. The process of authentication and the marking of a diagram can be seen in the following dialogue that takes place after the victim has testified he was robbed by the defendant:

Prosecutor:	Where did the robbery occur?
Witness:	Where I work, at Larry's Liquor, on 3957 McKinney Street.
Prosecutor:	Your honor, I request that this diagram, be marked as State's Exhibit 3 for identification purposes.
Judge:	It will be marked as Exhibit 3.
Prosecutor:	Mr. Witness, I want to call your attention to Exhibit 3, the large white diagram on the easel behind counsel table and ask if you can identify it?
Witness:	Yes. It's a diagram of the liquor store where I work.
Prosecutor:	How do you recognize it?
Witness:	I have worked there for four years.
Prosecutor:	Is it a fair and accurate depiction of the inside of the store where you worked?
Witness:	Yes, but it does not appear to be to scale.
Prosecutor:	Other than it being not to scale, does it show everything roughly where it is supposed to be?
Witness:	Yes.
Prosecutor:	Your honor, may the witness step down from the witness stand to mark the diagram.
Judge:	Yes, he may.
Prosecutor:	Please indicate by marking Exhibit 3 with the letter "W" where you were standing when you first saw the defendant on May 3, 2015.
Witness:	I was approximately here (marking the diagram with a large "W").

Prosecutor:	Now, would you please mark with the letter "D" where the defendant was when you first saw him?
Witness:	Yes.
Prosecutor:	Your honor, I would like to offer State's Exhibit 3 into evidence.
Judge:	Any objections?
Defense Attorney:	No, your honor.

Practice Pointer

An opposing attorney may attempt to mark on your exhibit during cross-examination of your witness or when questioning other witnesses. Although the trial court has discretion to allow this to occur, it is always best to ask the judge to keep this from happening on the basis that further marking will prevent the exhibit from correctly illustrating your witness's testimony.

B. Photographs

Like the predicate for maps, graphs, charts, and diagrams, the foundation for the admissibility of demonstrative photographs is having a witness testify that the exhibit "fairly and accurately" represents the scene depicted in the photograph at the time the photograph was taken. The witness need not be the photographer, the developer of the film, or someone who can testify about how the camera works or even the circumstances under which the photograph was taken. It can be anyone who has personal knowledge of what the photograph depicts.

Below is an example of how to lay the foundation for admission of a photograph of an accident scene:

Plaintiff's Attorney:	Ms. Plaintiff, I want to hand you what has been marked for identification as Plaintiff's Exhibit 5. Can you identify it?
Mrs. Plaintiff:	Yes. It is the intersection between Polk and Main Streets looking from the west.
Plaintiff's Attorney:	How can you recognize it?
Mrs. Plaintiff:	I am very familiar with this intersection because I have worked across the street from it for eight years.
Plaintiff's Attorney:	Does this photograph fairly and accurately represent the intersection of Polk and Main Streets as it looked on the day of your accident?
Mrs. Plaintiff:	Yes.

Plaintiff's Attorney:	Your honor, I now offer Plaintiff's Exhibit 5 into evidence.
Judge:	Any objections?
Defense Attorney:	No, your honor.
Judge:	Plaintiff's Exhibit 5 will be admitted into evidence.

The foundation for a photograph can be much more involved when there are no eyewitnesses to testify about whether the photograph is a fair and accurate representation of what it purports to be. Under such circumstances, more qualifying information must be provided concerning how the photograph was made, what it depicts, and why it is reliable.

III. EXERCISE: AUTHENTICATION OF EXHIBITS

The professor will assign students to perform specific tasks for the list of exhibits below. One or more students will lay the foundation for the exhibit through a witness they choose.[6] One or more students will be assigned to oppose the admission of the exhibit. One or more students will serve as judges to make rulings.

Proponents of the exhibit: check your sources in advance to enable you to list bullet points of the foundational elements. Be prepared also to explain the relevance of the exhibit under Rule 401—why you are offering it—and to withstand any attacks based on Rule 403, hearsay, etc.

Opponents: prepare to do the same; you can object on the ground of "insufficient foundation" if one or more elements of the foundation are missing—on relevance—on Rule 403—on hearsay, etc. Judges: you will have to do the same so that you are well prepared to rule.

1. For the prosecution in the criminal case: offer the photographs of the fire victims at pp. 37–39 (Ch. 3 on Rule 403).
2. For the prosecution in the criminal case: offer Defendant's Arrest and Conviction Record, Ex. B hereto, under two scenarios: (a) Defendant testifies; and (b) Defendant does not testify.

   [Defendant has told his counsel the following background to his two convictions:

   "I have two criminal convictions. The first one was in YR-9—I had just turned 20 and I celebrated by getting really drunk at a bar—yes, on a fake ID card—then got into a fight and got charged with assault or something like that. I realized I was in the wrong, so I pleaded guilty. I only got probation and community service, plus

---

[6] The available witnesses are: Nat Rogers, Frederica Rogers, Frank Derry, Thelma Derry, Investigating Police Officer Pat Lukasz, Lucia Beebe (owner/operator of Nova Hardware), and Fire Investigator Mark Crassus.

because I had been drinking pretty heavily since I was 15, the court ordered me to attend A.A. The second one was a tax evasion charge in YR-4—I made a mistake, thinking I could deduct a whole bunch of job-related expenses, so they threw the book at me, but that was only a misdemeanor. I pleaded guilty again to make it go away quick."]

3. For the defense in the civil case: offer the diagram showing the placement of the Rogers and Derry properties, Ex. C hereto. The Derry property is #305, and the Rogers property is # 307.
4. For the plaintiff in the civil case: offer the letter from Frederica, Ex. D hereto.
5. For the prosecution in the criminal case: offer the computer printout from Nova Hardware, Ex. E hereto.
6. For the prosecution in the criminal case: offer the video of the fire, Ex. F hereto.

EXHIBIT B

ARREST AND CONVICTION RECORD **Frank D. Derry**

Run Date: Dec. 3, YR-2

Run Time: 10:47 am

Request By: State Fire Investigator M. Crassus

NAM/01 DERRY, FRANK D.

NAM/02

NDL/C7837664

SOC/626536556

....

ARR/DET/CITE/CONV:

#1

04–18–YR-9 ARREST NPC 205—AGGRAVATED ASSAULT, FELONY

05–23–YR-9 CONVICTED, PLEA OF GUILTY, FELONY: SEN. 1 YEAR PROBATION, 60 DAYS COMMUNITY SERVICE, 6 MONTHS ATTEND A.A.

****

#2

10–23–YR-4 CIT. NPC 1437—TAX FRAUD—PERJURY, MISDEMEANOR

12–30–YR-4 CONVICTED, PLEA OF GUILTY, MISDEMEANOR: SEN. 6 MONTHS PROBATION

****

END OF RECORD

CERTIFIED AS A CORRECT COPY
FROM THE RECORD.
Attest: Luke D. Scrivener
Clerk, Criminal Division

EXHIBIT C

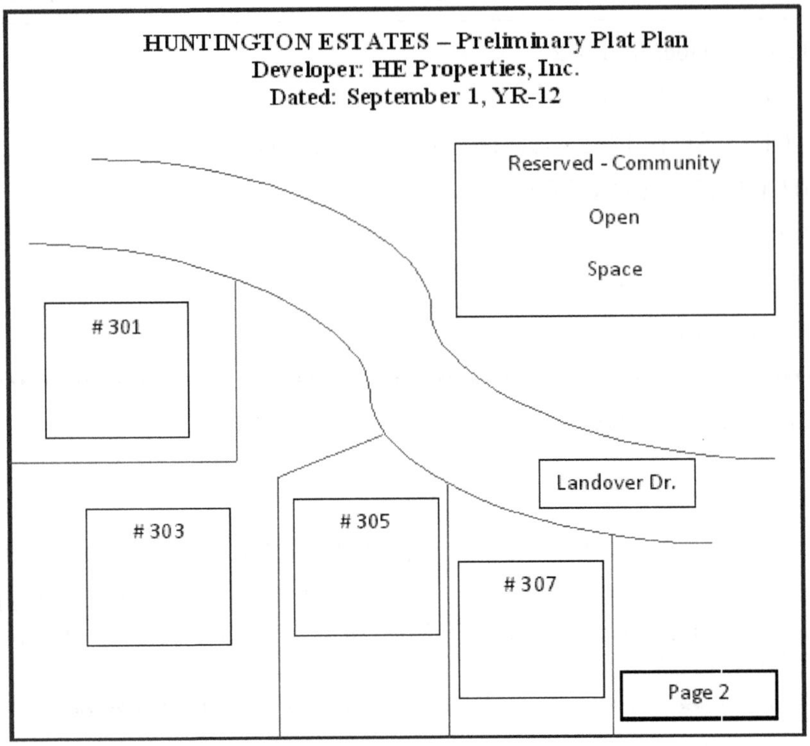
HUNTINGTON ESTATES – Preliminary Plat Plan
Developer: HE Properties, Inc.
Dated: September 1, YR-12
Reserved - Community
Open
Space
301
303
305
307
Landover Dr.
Page 2

EXHIBIT D

NUSQUAM STATE HOSPITAL
436 Serenity Drive
Novurbana, NU

Nat –

I don't know how much longer I can take this. I've been here for three weeks now, and the meds are really getting me down. The shrink says I have to take them, they are supposed to keep my spirits up, but for me they do just the opposite. I feel like giving up – I 'm sure that's why they don't give me any knives with my food or belts for my gown. They don't say so, but I know I'm on what they call "suicide watch."

All I really cared about was you and the kids and our beautiful home we worked so hard to buy and fix up, and now we're like homeless. You tell me to keep my hopes up --- for what?

F

EXHIBIT E

NOVA HARDWARE chmn678=9033447 – 1029YR-2 – page 1

Date	Item	No.	Customer	Amount
1029YR-2	½" dowel	3	Brill Builders	1.19
1029YR-2	Rubbermaid liner	6	Enriquez	10.49
1029YR-2	Kingsford Lighter	10	Derry	33.90
1029YR-2	Pumpkin Carve	1	Francis	3.89
1029YR-2	Kerosene – own can	2 gal	Brill Builders	7.30
1029YR-2	Cedar-O broom	1	White	10.59
1029YR-2	10d nails	1 lb	Handy Andy	2.40
1029YR-2	2x4 – 8′	14	Handy Andy	42.42
1029YR-2	Sheetrock – 4x8	3	Handy Andy	60.90
1029YR-2	Eveready AA – doz	1	Handy Andy	16.50

EXHIBIT F

http://www.youtube.com/watch?v=RJYRsmqayFo

[End of Exercise]

CHAPTER 11

FINAL EXERCISE

I. INTRODUCTION

For the final, "wrap-up" exercise you will watch a trial video in class. Your professor will assign roles to class members: prosecutors, defense attorneys, and judges. The video will be stopped for objections and discussion. In many cases the role-players on the video will not state objections they should ordinarily make; that omission is deliberate to give you (1) as opponent the opportunity to raise objections the role-players neglected to assert, and (2) as proponent the chance to advance arguments for the admission of the evidence. At other points, the video includes objections made by the "actors" and then a ruling on the objection by the on-screen "judge." However, do not assume that the ruling is necessarily correct. Your professor may pause the tape to give your in-class judge an opportunity to hear further argument (from *you*) and second-guess the ruling.

APPENDIX

CASE FILES

Appendix A—Criminal Case

ARSON

During the early morning hours of November 13, YR-2, a fire broke out in the home that Defendant Frank Derry shared with his wife Thelma and their three daughters. Thelma and the three girls were severely burned.

In the days following the fire a State arson investigator, Mark Crassus, concluded that the fire was caused by arson, largely because he says he found many signs of the use of "accelerant—flammable material/liquid used to start and spread a fire quickly." Crassus then partnered with local Police Department detectives to determine the perpetrator. The investigating team has charged Derry with arson, aggravated arson, and attempted murder. The prosecution's theory is that Crassus's investigation showed that arson caused the fire, and that Derry was the likely arsonist because (a) he was motivated by hostility towards Thelma and a fear of possible divorce and consequent alimony and child support orders against him, and (b) his behavior during the fire was inconsistent with that of a husband and father truly concerned with his family's safety.

Defendant has entered a plea of Not Guilty, placing on the prosecution the burden of proving each element of the charged offenses beyond a reasonable doubt. The criminal case is set for trial May 21, YR+1. The proposed Jury Instructions are as follows:

Arson. The defendant is charged with arson. To prove that the defendant is guilty of this crime, the State must prove that:

1. The defendant set fire to or burned a structure; and
2. He acted willfully or maliciously.

To *set fire to* or *burn* means to damage or destroy with fire either all or part of something, no matter how small the part.

Someone commits an act *willfully* when he or she does it willingly or on purpose.

Someone acts *maliciously* when he or she intentionally does a wrongful act or when he or she acts with the unlawful intent to defraud, annoy, or injure someone else.

Aggravated Arson. If you find the defendant guilty of arson, you must decide whether the State has proved the additional allegation that the arson was aggravated. To prove this allegation, the State must prove that:

1. The defendant acted willfully, maliciously, deliberately, and with premeditation; and
2. The defendant acted with intent to injure one or more persons, or to damage property under circumstances likely to injure one or more persons.

Attempted Murder. The defendant is charged with attempted murder. To prove that the defendant is guilty of attempted murder, the State must prove that:

1. The defendant took at least one direct but ineffective step towards killing another person, and
2. The defendant intended to kill that person.

A *direct step* requires more than merely planning or preparing to commit murder or obtaining or arranging for something needed to commit murder. A direct step is one that goes beyond planning or preparation and show that a person is putting his or her plan into action. A direct step indicates a definite and unambiguous intent to kill. It is a direct movement toward the commission of the crime after preparations are made. It is an immediate step that puts the plan in motion so that the plan would have been completed if some circumstance outside the plan had not interrupted the attempt.

Appendix B—Civil Case

ARSON - NEGLIGENCE - INTENTIONAL TORT

The facts set forth above for the Criminal Case are incorporated here by reference.

The house belonging to Derry's neighbor, Nat Rogers, caught fire from sparks carried by the wind from Derry's house to Rogers's. Rogers's house suffered major fire damage. Rogers and his wife Frederica have sued Derry on the grounds of (a) negligence and (b) intentional tort, the latter count with a prayer for punitive damages (which may be awarded in this jurisdiction for "willful, wanton disregard for another's life, safety, or property") based on the evidence that Derry set the fire at his house. The Rogers claims the following elements of damage: (1) monetary loss from the physical damage to their house, which was completely gutted by the fire and the fire-department's actions to quench the fire, (2) emotional distress caused to Rogers and his wife from the loss of their house and its contents, and (3) physical injuries Nat Rogers received when he tried to save personal items from the house before the fire department arrived.

Defendant has pleaded the defenses of (a) denial of the facts alleged and (b) comparative fault on the ground that Rogers did not take sufficient steps to prevent the damage to his property.

Defendant also filed a motion to dismiss under the Nita equivalent of FRCP 12, asserting that plaintiffs' claim for emotional distress failed to state a cause of action under Nita law, in that emotional distress from an event of property damage such as that alleged by plaintiffs is not recoverable unless the claimant proves that the distress was caused to one who was within the "zone of danger" at the time of the event. The court denied the motion without prejudice, stating that, while defendant's statement of the law was correct, the motion was premature, since the complaint sufficiently alleged facts to support a "zone-of-danger" claim. The court added that defendant could renew the motion after discovery or at trial depending on the proofs offered by plaintiffs.

The civil case is expected to go to trial in late Yr+1. The proposed jury instructions are as follows:

Basic Standard of Care. Negligence is the failure to use reasonable care to prevent harm to oneself or to others.

A person can be negligent by acting or by failing to act. A person is negligent if he or she does something that a reasonably careful person would not do in the same situation or fails to do something that a reasonably careful person would do in the same situation.

You must decide how a reasonably careful person would have acted in defendant's situation.

Intentional Tort—Punitive Damages. If you find that defendant's action or inaction in causing the harm that plaintiff alleges was intentional, you may, but are not required to, award punitive damages.

An action or inaction is *intentional* if the actor intended to cause the harm complained of or if he/she was substantially certain that such harm would result from his/her conduct.

Infliction of Emotional Distress—the "Zone of Danger: Rule. Plaintiffs have alleged and offered proofs of emotional distress they claim they suffered as a result of the fire at their house. To recover on this claim, plaintiffs must have proved to you by a preponderance of the evidence that at the time of the fire they were within the "Zone of Danger"—that is, they were in a location where the defendant's conduct could have caused physical harm to the plaintiffs.